An Introduction to Tracing Your German Ancestors

SECOND EDITION

Peter Towey

Published by
The Federation of Family History Societies (Publications) Ltd
Units 15-16 Chesham Industrial Centre,
Oram Street, Bury, Lancs BL9 6EN

in association with
The Anglo-German Family History Society

First published 1998
Second edition 2002

ISBN 1 86006 140 0

Printed and Bound by the Alden Group, London and Northampton.

Contents

Introduction

Some of you will know that you have German ancestors, who they were and where they came from. Many of you, however, will only suspect that the family's surname looks "German" or will know that an ancestor came from Germany but not where or when. This book aims to help all of you.

First of all, however, it is necessary to define what we mean by "German". There was no State called Germany until 1871. Before then there was a multiplicity of sovereign Kingdoms (eg Prussia, Bavaria, Saxony, Württemberg, Austria); Grand Dukedoms (eg Hesse, Baden); Dukedoms (eg Brunswick); many smaller states like Schaumburg-Lippe or Saxe-Coburg-Gotha, and even free city states like Hamburg, Frankfurt am Main, and Bremen. The relations of these states to each other, their boundaries and even their names and existence varied over time. The importance of this for the family historian is that each state kept its own records and had different laws about what needed to be recorded. Unlike England and Wales or Scotland there is no single place where all the records can be consulted. Even after Civil Registration covered the whole of pre First World War Germany in 1876, the records were not centralised but were kept in the local town hall. To do research in Germany, therefore, you need a good atlas! I intend, therefore, to deal with the German-speaking parts of Europe including Austria and Switzerland as well as the territories in the East that now form parts of Poland, the Ukraine and Russia; any part of this vast area could have been called "Germany" in the past.

Anyone who believes that they have German ancestry is urged to join the Anglo-German Family History Society which is a member of the FFHS and of the US-based Federation of Eastern European Family History Societies (FEEFHS). The Society was formed in 1987 by several English family historians who had discovered that they had German roots but had no idea how to research them. Since then it has sought out, indexed and, in some cases, published records that are likely to inform and help others in the same position. It has also published books on aspects of German life in the United Kingdom: on internment, on the

German churches, and on sugar bakers and other German occupations. If you are new to German research, someone in the Society has probably been there before you and should be able to advise. The quarterly magazine, "Mitteilungsblatt", itself has contained articles on many aspects of research and its Master Index is well worth a look. I should add that, despite its name, the magazine is in English!

It is also worth recording that the Society of Genealogists Library in London contains an excellent and growing collection of books that will be of great help to anyone researching their German ancestry. It is the best collection of such books available anywhere in the UK.

This book is divided into two parts: Part I deals with finding where in Germany or the German-speaking parts of Europe your ancestor came from and Part II deals with researching in the German-speaking parts of Europe. As it is quite impossible to do more than scratch the surface in a book of this size, there is a detailed annotated bibliography at the end.

I would like to take this opportunity of thanking all those who have helped me in putting this book together. I would like to acknowledge the assistance of the staff of the Public Record Office and London Metropolitan Archives for their help with their records; the members of the Anglo-German FHS who have taught me so much about German family history over the last 11 years; but, in particular, Roy Bernard for founding the Anglo-German FHS and nurturing it over its first decade; Len Metzner and Pam Freeman for giving so much of their time to tracking down, preserving and indexing records of Germans in UK; and Jenny Towey, my wife, and the Society's Secretary for its first 15 years, for encouraging me to write this book and putting up with me while I did so! Peter Towey, Teddington, May 1998.

Introduction to second edition
It is pleasant indeed to be asked to prepare a second edition of this booklet. Though it was specifically designed to help people researching their German-speaking ancestors in UK, I have heard from people in Australia, the USA and Canada who have found it useful; I am happy that it has been of some service. Since the first edition, many more useful sources and articles have become available and I have discovered more; I refer to many of them here. I hope that many more will become available over the next few years.

Thank you to those of you who diplomatically pointed out those errors that have been corrected; I would be grateful to hear of any others. Thank you also to my wife, Jenny, who cleared up around me while I was concentrating on updating this booklet, and who also proof-read it.

Peter Towey
Plymouth, Devon, January 2002

PART I

Tracing German Ancestors in England and Wales

An overview of the history of German Immigration

There have been Germans living in England, particularly London, since the beginning of our recorded history. Germany was, after all, only on the other side of the North Sea. When the thrones of England and Hanover were united in the person of King George I in 1714 many Hanoverians came with him and since then there has been a constant stream of German-speaking immigrants'.[1]

The records of the Army, Royal Navy and Royal Marines and even the East India Company testify to the numbers of young German men seeking their fortune in the British services. Many German princelings made their budgets balance by selling the regiments they raised into British service — the "Hessians" who fought for King George III in the American War of Independence are the best known but there were many others. During the French Revolutionary and Napoleonic Wars many more young men fled the invading French armies and took ship to England. Some trying to escape being pressed into Napoleons Armies ended up being pressed into the British Army or Navy! A whole army, the Hanoverian army, escaped en bloc and served as the Kings German Legion until Hanover was freed and the troops were able to go home in 1815.

In the 19th century the flow of immigrants from the German states increased as a result of many rulers' attempts to suppress democratic and nationalist feeling. After the failure of the 1848 democratic revolts, many academics and other middle class Germans came to London — many settling in Camberwell in Surrey.[2] But the main influx from the beginning of the century was of young Germans seeking their fortune in the main industrialized power of the Age and, especially, in the capital of the British Empire: London. This influx continued until the outbreak of the First World War in 1914. In the run up to, and during, the War people with Germanic names and Germanic accents were subject to hatred and mob violence and, after the Lusitania was sunk in 1915, German males of fighting age who had not become naturalized British citizens were interned. During and after the War many German nationals were forcibly repatriated and this really was the end of the pre-War German community. Because of their treatment in the War, many British people of German descent changed their names and tried to bury all trace of their German descent; in many cases they were all too successful and their descendants often do not realise that they have German ancestry until they start researching.

USING BRITISH RECORDS

The Census

Just because you have found an ancestor with a German name, it does not mean that he or she was born in Germany; my great great grandfather Wernint Weyman was actually born in Whitechapel in 1822. It was his father, Johann Friedrich Weyman, who was the immigrant. So you need to trace your ancestry through British records in the usual way until you find which one was an immigrant. The most usual way of discovering this in 19th century records is from the census. From 1851 onwards, the enumerator was required to record the birthplace of each individual. Sadly it was considered that the name of the Country of birth was enough if outside England and Wales so you often only find "Germany" or "Prussia" or "Hanover" in the "Where Born" column. Sometimes though you can be lucky and you get the name of the village or town. That is why it is even more essential than usual to trace your possibly-German ancestor through each of the censuses: 1851, 1861, 1871, 1881, 1891 and, when it is available from January 2002, 1901 - if the birthplace is given in just one of the censuses it will save you a great deal of searching.

The 1841 census does not even give the Country of birth but puts an "F" in the "Where Born" column meaning "born in Foreign Parts". This is better than nothing, however, as it is an indication that the person concerned was the immigrant. My Johann Friedrich Weymann, by then known by the very English-looking name of Frederick Weyman died in

10

1847 and it was only when I found him in the 1841 census that I realized that he was born a foreigner. His son, baptised Wernint Weyman at St Mary, Whitechapel, was known as William Weyman - to all appearances just as English as his father.

As with most records, there are a few conundrums about exactly what the placename recorded in the "Where born" column in the census actually means. Does "Hanover" mean the city or the Kingdom? What does "Germany" mean before 1871? Does "Germany, British Subject" mean that the individual had become a naturalized British Subject since being born in Germany or that they were the child of British subjects and just happened to be born in Germany? Even when you know what the description ought to have meant, how sure are you that the enumerator knew or cared? In many cases individuals noted as "Nat BS" (or "Naturalized British Subject") in a census do not appear to have been naturalized at all. Probably the immigrant, possibly with poor English, did not understand the census question and thought he was being asked if he was a loyal subject of the Queen.

Naturalization Records

The obvious records to go to, if you believe your ancestor was an immigrant, are the Home Office records at the Public Record office at Kew. The PRO has just (2000) brought out a useful addition to its series of Readers Guides: "Immigrants and Aliens",[3] which outlines the kind of records you might expect to find at Kew on your ancestors.

Until the First World War there was no legal requirement that aliens living in the United Kingdom must become naturalized. Many, indeed most, German and other aliens lived and died in the UK without naturalizing. Naturalization was an expensive business and for many there seemed to be no point. This was one of the reasons why so many who had lived in the UK for virtually all their lives were interned in the First World War and why they were so hurt and shocked by that treatment. The records can be so helpful, however, that it is always worth looking.

On the open shelves at Kew are the volumes of indexes of "Naturalization and Denization" running from 1509 to 1936. The indexes are not all entirely in alphabetical order and you should always be careful to check that you are looking in all the alphabetical sequences in the relevant volume. Be certain also to look for all possible spellings you can think of; foreign names are a particularly rich source of spelling variations.

As a rough guide, "Denization" is a cheaper form of naturalization; the Denizen could purchase land but not inherit it or hold public office; a Naturalized Subject had all the rights of someone born a British Subject. The indexes of records of Denization are in the same volumes as those of Naturalization but extend to 1873 only. Naturalization before 1844 involved getting a private Act of Parliament and, as you can imagine, was very expensive. If you find a reference in the indexes to an Act, you will find that they are not held by the PRO but by the House of Lords Record Office, House of Lords, London, SW1A 0PW, where they can be seen and/or copied. The relevant Home Office correspondence, however, where it survives, is in the PRO. Because of the expenses involved in getting a Private Act and, no doubt, the parliamentary time they used up, an Act was passed enabling the Home Secretary to grant naturalization certificates without the need for a Private Act. This system came into use in 1844 and was the only system used after 1900.

During the period 1844 to 1900, a naturalization is more likely to be under this administrative procedure than by Private Act. If you are interested in the period after 1800, you should ask the staff at the desk in the Research Enquiries Room for their free leaflet *6. How to find and use Denization and Naturalization Records after 1800*".[4] Using this leaflet and the indexes, you can order up and photocopy the Home Office correspondence file. Before 1844, or where a private Act of Parliament is involved, there is not always a lot of personal information; though it is always worth looking for it. After 1844, the file normally contains the applicant's "Memorial" giving his personal details: place of birth, age or actual birth date, parents' names (often including the mother's maiden name) and the parents nationality. The papers also give the address(es) where the applicant had been living for the previous five years or more, his occupation and, often, the name of the firm for which he has been working. If he was married to a foreign wife, her name and details, the date and place of marriage and the names and ages of the children under 21 years old and the addresses where they are living (if different from the fathers address) are often given. This is because they too were covered by his naturalization. There should also be the affidavits by five or more British Subjects saying how long they had known him and that he was a fit and proper person to be given British Nationality. There will also be the report by the police saying he was a good citizen. As a general rule, the later the naturalization, the more information you can hope to find.

It is worth noting that these Home Office records include all denizations and naturalizations in the whole of the United Kingdom (ie England, Ireland, Scotland and Wales) from 1801 to 1922. After 1922, the Republic of Ireland had its own records which are in the Public Record Office in Dublin but the post 1922 records for Northern Ireland are with the other UK records at Kew.

While the Home Office correspondence files after 1922 and the more recent duplicate naturalization certificates after 1960 are currently closed to the public, if you are interested in a naturalization after those dates, it is often worth writing to the Departmental Record Officer, Home Office, Record Management Services, 50 Queen Anne's Gate, London, SW1H 9AT, and asking for the closure of the file to be reviewed. The DRO will consult the files and, if there appears to be no good reason why not, will tell the PRO to let you see and copy the file. This can, however, take some months; so be patient!

Before 1800

The indexes to Denizations and Naturalizations In England, Scotland, Wales and Ireland before 1800 are handily available in the published volumes of the Quarto Series of the Huguenot Society of Great Britain and Ireland and available in most large reference libraries.[5] However, the records of naturalizations in Scotland before the Union in 1707 do not appear to be included in the indexes. If you are interested in a person who may have been naturalised in Scotland before 1707, the records should be in the Scottish Record Office in:

(i) letters of naturalization in the Register of the Privy Seal (mainly for the late 16th century);
(ii) petitions recorded in the Register of the Privy Council; or
(iii) letters patent under the Great Seal.

I know of no indexes to these naturalizations so you just have to take pot luck!

Records of Aliens

In theory there was some control of aliens in the UK from the late 18th century but very few records relating to individuals survive. One early document is the Plymouth Aliens List[6] covering Jewish aliens living in Plymouth in Devon in 1798 and updated in 1803. Most of the 58 aliens listed were from places that were later in Germany. The list survived in the records of the Jewish Congregation in Plymouth and it could be that there are other similar lists in other archives in the UK. Please let me know if you find any.

A Central Registry of Aliens was set up in 1914 but the Central Register itself no longer survives. Each local Police Force kept details of all registered aliens in their area. Those aliens who were not interned were required to report weekly to their local police station. Unfortunately 99.99% of the records once kept locally have been destroyed, usually by the relevant Police Force which had nowhere to keep the records! Some surviving aliens' registration cards for the (London) Metropolitan Police area have survived and are being made available on microfiche at the PRO in Class MEPO35. They relate to only about 1,000 aliens and cover 1884-1989 (ie the date of arrival in UK) but with a large proportion from around the 1930s. It is usually advisable to check in the local Police Museum or County Record Office covering the area where "your" alien lived to see if any records have survived.

From 1934 the Home Office kept a single series of Aliens Personal Files covering all aliens coming to the UK for more than 3 months - not just those who naturalized. These files ceased when the individual died, finally left the Country or was naturalized. Where there was a pre-1934 file for the individual this was attached to and kept with the new file. These files were supposed to have been destroyed routinely after ceasing to be administratively relevant but some have survived and are still in the Home Office and will be transferred to the PRO in due course. For those aliens who were naturalized, the Home Office copy of the Naturalization Certificate is seen as the main record and these all survive. However, about 40% of the naturalization files created between 1934 and 1948 also still survive and are being moved to the PRO over the next 10 years or so. They will be in class HO 405 and an index will in due course be available on the PRO website on the Internet. So far (in 2001) only about 2,000 have been indexed and these are for those with surnames beginning with "A".

14

The files are closed for 100 years but, in the meantime, the Home Office Departmental Record Officer will answer postal enquiries on them on the same basis as above. I understand that the future of the post-1948 aliens files is being reviewed by the Home Office.

German Churches in the UK

If you have drawn a blank with the census and the naturalization records, another source that could give you the place of origin of your immigrant ancestor is the records of the German churches in the United Kingdom. The registers of all the churches listed below, with the exception of Christchurch, Kensington, the Chapel Royal at St Jamess Palace, and the Rev Schultze's registers from Dublin, have been included in the Anglo-German FHS Names Index (qv).

London

So many German-speakers moved to live and work in London that, from the 17th century, there have been Protestant churches in London holding services in German.[7] Most of the Germans coming to London were Protestants because the neighbouring parts of Germany, from which most immigrants came, were mainly Protestant and also because, for much of the time, Catholics would have got a better reception in other Countries.

It was not uncommon for Germans in South East England to travel relatively long distances to attend services in their own churches and in their own language. These churches sometimes kept records of where their church members had come from in Germany and this is often noted in their records - the "Kirchenbücher", Church Books or parish registers, or even in the Pastor's notebooks kept with the individual church's general records. Two of the Anglo-German FHS's most indefatigable workers, Len Metzner and Pam Freeman, are gradually working through the records of all the German churches in England indexing the registers and locating, identifying and listing the other records.

The main German Protestant churches are the Lutheran and the Reformed or Calvinist Churches. Both are represented among the churches in London. The earliest were the Lutheran churches. The "Hamburger-Lutherische Kirche" or "Hamburg Lutheran Church" opened its doors in Little Trinity Lane in the City in 1669. It moved to Dalston in

Hackney, next to the German Hospital, in the 1870s and the records are at the Guildhall Library - besides the copies of the pre 1837 registers held among the non-conformist registers in Class RG3 at the Family Record Centre (FRC) in Myddleton Street.

Another contemporary Lutheran church was St Marienkirche or "St Mary in the Savoy"[8] which was in the Liberty of the Savoy just off the Strand. Its name has now been transferred to the chapel in the basement of the International Lutheran Students Centre in Sandwich Street, St Pancras. There are copy registers, in the FRC in Class RG3, for 1669 to 1840.

The next Lutheran church was St George's Lutheran Church in Little Alie Street, Aldgate, which was opened in 1763 and still exists. It was specifically intended to serve the growing community of German sugar bakers in the East End. Sadly, declining congregations caused its closure as a church in November 1996 but the building has been taken over by the Historic Chapels Trust and it is to be preserved. There should be the occasional service there in German from time to time. If you want to see what an 18th or 19th century German Lutheran church looked like, you should arrange a visit. The box pews and the memorial tablets in German and English survive. The congregation has, however, been merged with that of St Marienkirche in St Pancras and the records of both churches have been deposited in Tower Hamlets Library. The Anglo-German FHS has indexed and published the registers of St George's from 1763 to 1895,[9] though the registers do extend to the present day and an index to the registers after 1895 is in Tower Hamlets Library.

We have been less lucky with the German Reformed Church records. A German Reformed church opened in the Savoy in 1697. It moved several times: to an old Huguenot chapel in Dutchy Street, in 1771; when that was demolished in 1816 to make way for the approach to Waterloo Bridge, it moved to Hooper Square, Aldgate, from 1816 to 1887; and, when that building was purchased for a railway goods yard, to a purpose-built church in Goulston Street, Whitechapel, from 1887 until it was, ironically, bombed in the second World War. The church was not replaced and the post War congregation shared St George's with the Lutheran congregation. The moves have not been kind to the records and all that survives dates from 1824 - the records of the previous 127 years have disappeared. The surviving records are at Tower Hamlets Library with St George's and an index to the surviving registers has been published by the Anglo-German FHS.[10] A history of 300 years of the German Reformed church in London is in preparation but, in the meantime, the best history is an article by the same author in the Anglo-German FHS magazine "Mitteilungsblatt".[11]

A German Roman Catholic Church, dedicated to the English monk that converted the heathen Germans: St Boniface, was opened in Whitechapel in 1862. Before that there was a German Catholic Chapel in London from 1812. The records (baptisms from 1812 and marriages from 1862) are still at the church; rebuilt in modern style after being bombed in the Second World War. Most of the German Catholics in London at the time appear to have come from the nearer Roman Catholic parts of Germany: the Rhineland, the Palatinate (Pfalz), Baden and Württemberg with only a few from Bavaria proper and Austria. But be careful, one of the Anglo-German FHS members has found that, even after St Boniface's church was founded, her German Roman Catholic ancestors had at least one of their children baptised at St George's Lutheran Church. The churches are less than a mile apart so it can hardly have been a question of not being able to get to St Boniface. So if you cannot find an entry in the records of St Boniface, try St George's.

Before these special churches were built, and even afterwards when it suited them, German-speakers worshipped in the local Church of England parish churches or in other suitable churches. Lutheran worship was probably close enough to that of the Church of England for it not to worry either party. Many Reformed church members probably went to one of the many English non-conformist churches around and the Catholics went, like other Catholics, to where they could find a Catholic priest: you should look for their records among the other English Roman Catholic records of the period.

The earlier German churches were set up by the merchants and other middle class Germans but were open to all classes. However, the aristocracy tended to live in the West End and you will find many of them attending the churches in the Court suburbs of Kensington, Kew, etc. But you will also find them in the German Lutheran Chapel Royal in the Palace of St James, founded in 1700 by Queen Anne, whose husband Prince George of Denmark was a Lutheran.[12] The registers from 1712 to 1836 are among the Non-Conformist registers in the FRC (in Class RG4/4568 & 4569) and I understand that those from 1866 onwards are in another German church: Christuskirche, Montpelier Place, Kensington, London SW7. Unfortunately the Anglo-German FHS has not yet had access to that German church (which also has records of its own) and the registers are not indexed.

The public was also often allowed to use the various Embassy chapels from at least the 17th century onwards. That there are registers existing for various Catholic Chapels, like the Bavarian and Sardinian Embassy Chapels, is well known, but there were also Lutheran and Reformed Church Chapels. For example the Prussian Embassy Chapel in the 17th century had a Lutheran chaplain and it is probable that other German Embassies or Legations, besides the Swedish and Danish Embassies, had Lutheran or Calvinist chaplains. I have no idea where any of these chapels registers, if any survive, may be and would welcome information.

The German middle classes up to the end of the 18th century tended to live in and around the City and they were catered for by the Hamburg Lutheran Church and St Mary in the Savoy. The German working classes, especially the sugar bakers that started settling in London in the mid to late 18th century, tended to live and work in Whitechapel and Stepney. The church of St George in Alie Street was specifically built for the sugar bakers of Whitechapel and Aldgate and, over the next 150 years, the large working class German community in East London used it. Many, however, especially those that married English girls, used the Church of England parish churches: the registers of St Mary, Whitechapel, and St George in the East are full of German names. My own Weyman family, Johann Friedrich having married an English girl in St Mary, Whitechapel, had all the children baptised in one or other of those two churches. However, as he got older, his thoughts must have returned to his German roots for his burial in 1847 appears in the register of the German Reformed church: St Paul, Hooper Square. Perhaps he attended the German services there while his wife and children attended the Church of England?

As the 19th century progressed, the German community in London increased considerably, those who had done well in business moved out to the new suburbs and new, well-off, middle class refugees arrived. This led to the founding of new German churches in the suburbs: the Camberwell Evangelical Church in 1854; the Islington Lutheran Church in 1856 and the Sydenham Evangelical Church (now called the Dietrich Bonhoeffer Evangelical Church) in 1875.

England and Wales outside London
In most cases there were no German churches and you must look for Germans' baptisms, marriages and burials in the usual places. For example there was a large influx of German miners from Augsburg into Cornwall, South Wales and Cumbria in the 16th century. The Germans appear in the local registers from then on; especially in Keswick and Coniston where a relatively large German group settled and was gradually absorbed into the local community over the centuries.[13] Similarly a large group of swordmakers from Solingen came to Shotley Bridge in co. Durham in the 1680s to make sword blades for the British Army and their names appear in the local registers for generations after.[14]

It was not until the mid 19th century that German Protestant churches (I do not know of any German Catholic churches outside London) started appearing outside London. Those that I am aware of are: Liverpool, founded 1846; Hull, Yorkshire, founded 1848; Manchester, founded 1855; Sunderland, co. Durham, founded 1863; Bradford, Yorkshire, founded 1876; South Shields, co. Durham, founded 1879; and Newcastle upon Tyne, founded 1906. It is clear from the locations that many were intended to serve the German merchant seamen and the craftsmen, tradesmen and merchants who settled in the sea ports or where the cotton and woollen industries were booming. In many cases, besides the church registers, other records have survived and there are even some published histories.[15]

Ireland
A German Lutheran church was founded in Marlborough Street in Dublin in 1697 moving to a purpose built church in Poolbeg Street in 1725 where it remained for the next 100 years. The community appears to have disappeared by 1850, when the church burned down, and it was not until 1930 that German services were held again in Dublin.[16] Sadly I have no knowledge of what happened to the records of this church other than two baptism and marriage registers of the Rev Schultze covering 1806-37 which are held by the Registrar-General for Ireland in Dublin (and contain many irregular marriages). I know of no other German churches in Ireland. It is likely that wherever Germans settled in Ireland they used the local parish churches and it is there that you should look for their baptisms, marriages and burials, if those registers still survive. Even where there were large settlements, as with the Palatines of 1710 who

settled on Sir Thomas Southwell's estate at Rathkeale, co. Limerick, and on the estate of Abel Ram at Gorey, co. Wexford, the settlers used the local Church of Ireland parish churches - at least until Methodism provided an alternative.

Scotland

I am only aware of one German church in Scotland: the German Protestant church in Edinburgh. The records are in the Scottish Record Office and baptism and burial registers survive from 1884 and Confirmation and Marriage Registers from 1885. The Church was there much earlier, from 1862, and there is also a list of members from 1864 to 1885, and other records surviving from the 1870s.

Jewish Records

Many immigrants, particularly in the mid to late 19th century and in the 20th century were Jewish - see the reference to the Plymouth Aliens List 1798 & 1803 above. They should appear in the same civil sources as gentile immigrants but, in place of the church records, they should be sought in the records of the synagogues. I will not try to cover Jewish research, not having much experience in that field, but recommend the books in the bibliography.[17] If you cannot find your German ancestor in UK in the period before civil registration, it is worth considering whether they may have been Jewish originally. Some, like Benjamin Disraeli's father, were converted to Christianity and many married gentile wives or husbands.

Records of the British Armed Services
The Army

The records of the British Army, Royal Navy and Royal Marines are full of German names. The British Crown often hired regiments of German mercenary soldiers to serve in its armies during wartime. The Hessians and Waldeckers of the American War of Independence are some of the better known examples. In such cases the regiment was generally hired as a unit and the Treasury paid the money direct to the German Prince concerned; any surviving records of individuals, therefore, would be in Germany. Up to 1794, individual Germans and other foreigners could enlist in British regiments: for example it was quite fashionable in the 18th century for British regiments to have German drill sergeants. The law did not allow the setting up, as part of the British Army, of regiments composed wholly or mainly of foreigners. There were, however, some British Regiments, like the 60th Foot, to which individual German, Swiss, and other foreign-born recruits were usually posted. The law was changed in 1794 and allowed the raising of "auxiliary" regiments from foreign-born recruits. These included many Germans. In these cases the regiments were part of the British Army and the records are at the PRO, Kew.[18]

The main component of German troops in the British Army during the Napoleonic Wars was the King's German Legion (KGL). It was formed when the Electorate of Hanover (of which King George III was the Elector) was conquered by Napoleon in 1803. The Royal Hanoverian Army was disbanded but large numbers escaped to England where in August 1803 they were reformed into the KGL. They served in most of the theatres of war including the Peninsula and, most famously, at Waterloo where they distinguished themselves, especially in the defence of La Haye Sainte. They were disbanded as part of the British Army and returned to Hanover where they were recreated as the Royal Hanoverian Army in 1815. While in exile they were stationed in England: the main base being at Bexhill, Sussex, the cavalry at Ipswich, Suffolk, and the engineers at Weymouth, Dorset.[19] The records are voluminous and have largely been indexed by Len Metzner for the Anglo-German FHS Names Index (qv). Many of the records that went back with them to Hanover, including the pension records, were being indexed by the late Jürgen Ritter and have been published by the local German family history society in Hanover.[20]

The British Government was raising regiments of foreigners as late as the outbreak of the Crimean War in 1854. The British German Legion, made up mainly of Germans and Belgians, was first based at Shorncliffe in Kent for training in early 1855. The first troops left for the Crimea in October 1855. Even after the armistice was signed in April 1856, German recruits continued to arrive. In July 1856 the British German Legion was marched to other barracks: some to Aldershot in Hampshire and some to Colchester in Essex to be disbanded and repatriated. Most went back to Germany or joined other Countries' Armies. However, the British Government wanted to recruit some of them to the Cape Colony Police for South Africa. These jobs were supposed to be for married men only so there was a flurry of marriages of German soldiers to English girls. In

Colchester Garrison Church there were 150 such marriages in October 1856 - 64 of them on one day: 20th October 1856.[21] The records of the British German Legion are among the War Office records in the PRO, Kew. Some of the Germans were also recruited from England and from Cape Colony to help to put down the Indian Mutiny and they appear among the records of the Indian Army in the British Library's India Office Library and Records, which are in the new British Library building at St Pancras.

The Royal Navy and Royal Marines
The Royal Marine and Royal Navy records contain details of large numbers of Germans at all periods before the late 19th century. There are no records that specifically deal with Germans but the records are generally good and many ships, particularly during the Napoleonic Wars, had a number of foreigners on board - sometimes Germans. There is no consolidated index and you have to look through the individual ship's Muster Book and Description Book where they survive. These give the mans' age and place of birth; often giving the actual town or village. Royal Marine Description Books contain the same details.[22]

The Merchant Navy
Many Germans served as seamen, mates and Masters in the British Merchant Marine. This was often, no doubt, because the British Merchant Marine offered sailors a wider choice of berths than the German equivalent. Again there are no special records that relate solely to Germans and you have to use the records of the Registrar General of Shipping and Seamen now at the PRO, Kew.[23] These records really only start in the 1830s but there are earlier records relating to apprenticeships from 1824. There is a gap in the records of individuals between 1857 and 1913 but those from 1913 are now available on microfilm at the PRO, Kew. If you know the name of the ship your ancestor sailed on you can, with some detective work, consult the Crew Lists which give the ages and places of birth of each of the crew; or, if the seaman you are interested in was a Mate or a Master, there are good records available at the PRO, Kew and in the Guildhall Library. Against the general rule that only the wealthier immigrants are likely to have bothered with naturalization, it is worth checking in the case of merchant seamen from the latter 19th

century as there were special rules allowing them to naturalize without paying. You also often get a list of all the British ships they had sailed on for the previous seven years or so.

Hon. East India Company

I have already mentioned that some of the men of the British German Legion helped with the putting down of the Indian Mutiny in 1857 and can be found among the records of the Indian Army. India was also a magnet to Germans at other periods: as soldiers, merchants, explorers, missionaries, seamen or even as civil servants. The records of the East India Company (and, after 1861, the British Government of India) Army, Navy, Merchant Navy and Civil Service and the ordinary records of the births, marriages and deaths of Christians in the sub-continent are available at the British Library's India Office Library and Records, in Euston Road, St Pancras.[24]

The Palatines of 1709

The largest early influx of Germans to England was that of the "Poor Palatines" in 1709. The British Government of the time wanted to encourage the settlement of Protestants in New England to act as a buffer against the threat of the Catholic French, in Quebec. They decided to encourage poor Protestant Germans from the Palatinate (the Pfalz), to come to England before being shipped to New York. The response was much larger than they had expected and poor Germans arrived at Rotterdam in their thousands. The Treasury lists of the Germans being shipped from Rotterdam and those landed in London over the summer of 1709 survive.

There were 30,000 Germans, men, women and children, camped on Blackheath over much of the winter of 1709. The British Government changed while this was going on and the new Government had less interest in the scheme but the Germans were there and needed to be looked after. In the end some were shipped to New England, some settled in Ireland, over half (including all the Catholics!) appear to have been sent back to Germany, and some probably stayed in London and merged into the local population. I have not actually discovered anyone with a proven descent from a Palatine who stayed in England and would be very interested to hear from anyone who has.[25]

Ship's Passenger Lists and Aliens' Certificates

In most cases passengers arriving in England from German or other European ports were not recorded, or the records were not kept, until about the mid 19th century. However, in the PRO at Kew in the Home Office records are Ships Lists of Aliens (HO3/1-102) which cover the period 1836 to 1860 & 1867 to 1869 and give the alien's name, trade and place of birth/origin. These lists were deposited by the ships' masters on the ship's arrival in a UK port. There is a partial index to these records from 1847 to 1852, again by Len Metzner, which can be searched in the PRO or through the Anglo-German FHS; the index covers all those entries that gave a German place as the origin of the individual but some of the entries were illegible and, obviously, are not included. In HO2 are Aliens' Certificates for the period 1836 to 1852 which are kept under the port of arrival in Great Britain. They give the alien's nationality, profession, date of arrival, last Country visited and his signature There is an index in HO5/25-32 which covers the Aliens Certificates issued between 1826 and 1849. The certificates from 1826 to 1835 have not survived but the index itself can be helpful in indicating when and where an immigrant arrived here. Len Metzner has indexed HO2/213-228 covering all of 1852 and the returns for London and Folkestone for 1851, subject to the same caveats as HO3 above, so the only year missing from an index is 1850 and the returns from Dover for 1851. Len Metzner's indexes are in the Anglo-German FHS Names Index (qv).

German Occupations

German immigrants were, of course, as likely as the next immigrant to turn their hands to whatever work was available. However, you should not expect to find a German immigrant as eg a farm labourer in the English Midland shires, unless he was a POW in WWII and stayed on. At particular times, German immigrants were heavily represented in particular occupations. I have already mentioned the miners that came over to Cornwall, South Wales and Cumberland in the 16th century and the armed services in the Napoleonic period. Less obvious was the effective monopoly Germans had on the sugar industry, especially in London, from the mid 18th century to the mid 19th century. By the mid 19th century Stepney and Whitechapel in London were heavily populated by German-born sugar bakers; in the 1851 census you find whole streets where the adults were all born in Germany and the males are "sugar bakers" or "scum boilers" or some such term. These were the labourers who were willing to work long hours in dangerous and debilitating circumstances for relatively low pay. Contrary to some family traditions sugar bakers were not confectioners (though many of those were Germans too!) but people who worked in factories manufacturing sugar from the raw sugar cane that came in through the docks.[26]

The German Hospital at Dalston in Hackney was at the forefront of providing free medical treatment for the London poor (and not just Germans) and also pioneered high quality training for nurses in England. Florence Nightingale did some of her training there. The hospital was closed by the British Government during the Second World War and taken over by the NHS when it was set up after the War. The buildings still survive though they are no longer used by the NHS and have been converted into flats.[27]

Large numbers of Germans also became bakers (by the beginning of the First World War, a large proportion of the bakers in London had German names and questions were asked in Parliament about it!); pork butchers; ladies' and gentlemen's hairdressers (does anyone know why?); merchant seamen; and musicians (eg Handel, C. P. E. Bach, the Halle Orchestra, the Carl Rosa Opera Company, and the many groups of itinerant German bands and street orchestras that enlivened the British Victorian and Edwardian street scene).[28]

Internment
First World War
The First World War, and the anti-German hysteria that led up to it, largely destroyed the Victorian and Edwardian high tide of German immigration.[29] The use of internment against all Enemy Alien males between 18 and 65, fully enforced after the sinking of the Lusitania in 1915, led to the break up of families. The accompanying deportation or repatriation of old people, wives and children removed the remnants of the community. Even after the War when some families returned, it was still very unpopular to be, look or sound German and the community has not returned to its 19th century peak until recently. The trauma was such that, even to this day, some of the older members of the Anglo-German FHS want their membership kept secret for fear of reprisals. Fortunately

this is breaking down now and some members have even changed their surnames back to the German originals their grandparents tried to hide in 1914-19.[30]

The individual files of the First World War internees (usually known as "civilian POWs") have been largely destroyed by the Home Office though a few have been kept at the PRO as examples. The surviving files do not hold a great amount of useful information so their destruction may not be as great a loss as we might have thought; except that we now have no complete list of internees. There were lists of the internees produced by the British Government during the War: one copy for the "Protecting Power" to pass on to the enemy Government (ie Germany, Austria-Hungary, Bulgaria or Turkey), one for the Red Cross, and one to be kept by the British Government. The Red Cross copy is, we understand, complete but is now kept in Geneva. Until recently it was closed to research but the International Red Cross is now willing to undertake research in it. Their address is: ICRC Archives 19 Avenue de la Paix, CH-1202, Geneva, Switzerland. You can write in English. They charge 80 Swiss Francs an hour for research but you should not send any money with your initial enquiry. Experience of this service to date has not been good: they have failed to find details of POWs who they were known in the 1980s to have records for. It could be that their indexing system is not very good and you should not invest too much hope in them. It is, however, always worth trying! The British Government copy, so far as I have been able to ascertain, was kept at the Prisoner of War Information Bureau in London where it was destroyed with all the other records in an air raid in WWII.

The Anglo-German FHS found a large number of lists in the Federal German Archives in Koblenz, copied them and has indexes available for searching (in the Names Index (qv)). However those lists only run from 1916 to 1919 and only relate to the changes in status of the internees; names and addresses, ages and places of birth, etc. do not appear in 99% of cases presumably because those details are on the earlier, missing, lists. They also include a list of those German civilian POWs for whom the Prisoner of War Information Bureau held property so that, after the War, those POWs could claim their property back. As I have already mentioned the POW Information Bureau records were all destroyed but the list is useful. Incidentally you do sometimes find post-war wills of Germans in the English wills indexes where the executor is the POW Information Bureau.

The Koblenz Archives do not know where the earlier lists are nor do the Home Office or the PRO. The Koblenz lists are probably the set forwarded to the German Government through the Protecting Power. From 1914 until she entered the War on the Allied side in 1917, that Protecting Power was the United States. After that the Protecting Power was Switzerland. There may well be some records in the Swiss Government Archives but inquiries have not, to date, been successful. There does not appear to be anything useful in the US Archives.

The main prison camps for Civilian POWs in the First World War were at Knockaloe and Douglas in the Isle of Man. There are few traces there today but the Isle of Man Museum and Archives in Douglas do have a representative collection of papers and artefacts.[31] There was a considerable number of internment and transit camps elsewhere in the UK. The main camp in London was at Alexandra Palace where the London POWs were collected and sorted before being moved to the Isle of Man. Many appear to have stayed there permanently during the War.[32] In 1998 the Anglo-German FHS unveiled a plaque to the First World War internees at the site of Knockaloe Camp and in 2000 a similar plaque was unveiled at Alexandra Palace. A full list of First World War POW Camps in the British Empire, including their code letters as used in the Koblenz lists (above), was published at the time by the POW Information Bureau and has recently been reprinted by the Imperial War Museum.[33]

Second World War

During the Second World War the fate of Aliens was different. Civilian Aliens (including women) were arrested at the commencement of the war in September 1939, and many were transported to camps in Canada and elsewhere. After the sinking of the SS "Arandora Star" by a U-boat in July 1940, internees were kept in camps in UK, including the Isle of Man. However, because large numbers of the internees were Jewish and other refugees from Nazi oppression, Internment Tribunals were set up to separate Nazi sympathisers from the others. The record cards, dating from 1939 to 1947, are available on microfilm in PRO Class HO396: "Aliens Department: Internees Index", and contain useful personal information such as date and place of birth, address, occupation, etc. Where the Tribunal decided that the alien did not need to be interned, the full record card is available; where they were to be interned, the Tribunal's reasons are on the back of the card and you would need to apply to the Home Office for permission to see those details.

"Living with the Wire" covers internment in the Isle of Man during the Second World War too. Interest is also growing in internment in UK during and after the War when there were 1,500 Camps holding half a million men (though mainly military POWs). Dr J. Anthony Hellen has written a very useful article outlining the history, geography and nature of the camps and is currently working on a full-scale book.[34] He was consultant to the award-winning BBC2 TV programme "The Germans We Kept" in 2000 and he points out that English Heritage are now taking more interest in preserving surviving evidence of the camps.

Anglo-German FHS Names Index

As mentioned several times above and below, the Anglo-German Family History Society has, over the years, built up a large computerised Names Index which currently contains well over 500,000 entries, principally of Germans in UK. The sources used are various including most of the church registers of the German churches in England and Scotland; the records in the PRO of the King's German Legion; many Alien's records from the PRO, and many other miscellaneous sources. It includes all the indexes which Len Metzner has compiled over the years.[35] The Index is only available for use by members of the Society but, as you can imagine, is well worth a search.

Other Miscellaneous Sources

The Germans seem to have put more weight on providing a good education for their children than most contemporary English people. The churches were the main providers of education and as early as 1708 there was a German school attached to the German church of St Mary in the Savoy.[36] There was also a "poor house" provided nearby. The records of those bodies do not appear to survive in any amounts. Records do however survive for the St George's German Lutheran Church, Alie Street, boys' and girls' Infants School. The school buildings adjoined the church in Alie Street and were converted into flats in 1998-99. The records from 1828 to 1917 (when the school was closed by the British Government) have been indexed by Len Metzner and are available for searches in the Anglo-German FHS Names Index (qv). The records of the Society of the

Ladies' Charity of St George's German Lutheran Church, effectively out-relief for members of the German community who had fallen on hard times, also survive for 1821-1846 and 1868-1863 and are also indexed in the Names Index (qv).

IF YOU STILL DO NOT KNOW WHERE THEY CAME FROM

If, even after checking in the sources outlined above, you still do not know where your immigrant ancestor came from, there are some ways in which you can narrow the field of search.

Surnames

Like English surnames, German surnames can be very localised and in some cases can provide the clue you need to trace your immigrant ancestor. If you think that your surname is unusual it is worth looking in a German surname dictionary in case it is predominantly from a single area.[37] A factor that often throws newcomers to German research is that, in some cases, the surname of a wife or daughter is given the feminine ending "-in". Thus Rocker becomes Rockerin, Müller becomes Müllerin and Treuten becomes Treutenin. Where the surname already ends in "-in", "er" is inserted instead so that Schwecklin becomes Schwecklerin. These changes to the form of surnames, however, are not common in present-day Germany.

Telephone Directories

You can also look in the German telephone directories. I would not recommend looking in the individual volumes as, unlike British directories, each town or village is listed in a separate alphabetical sequence so that you need to know the actual place of residence before you can use them; not much use for our purposes. There is now, however, the alternative of the German Telephone Directory on CD-ROM. That provides a single alphabetical sequence as well as their usual place indexes and can be searched in a number of ways. The Anglo-German FHS has an up-to-date CD-ROM and will undertake searches for a small fee (they also hold the Austrian and Swiss Telephone Directories on CD-ROM). They are also available on the Internet.

If you can localise the name it may be worth writing to the local City or Town Hall and seeing what happens. This has been fruitful in the past: an immigrant called "August Trepte" was found in the 1851 census to have been born in Saxony - rather a large place! Looking in the CD-ROM the surname was found to be most common around Leipzig. Even though the immigrant probably arrived in London in the 1830s, a fax was sent to the City Archives (Stadtarchiv) in Leipzig who, by return, sent full details of the family being sought. This would, of course, only work with a relatively rare and localised surname. Incidentally the Christian name "August" would have pointed towards Saxony anyway as it was the name of many of the Kings of Saxony.

Another use of the CD-ROM, especially where the immigrant arrived in the last 100 to 150 years, is to obtain addresses of other people with the same surname and write to them. This has provided the big breakthrough in several cases that I know of but again is only really practicable if you know the region of origin and the surname is rare or localised enough for the numbers to be manageable.

Genealogical Dictionaries
It is not true to say that, where a surname starts with "von", it generally means that the family was ennobled. In many cases it is just a locative surname. However, when a person was ennobled in Germany they normally added a "von" to their surname so it could be a pointer. Also the surname does not have to be a placename; "von" could be put in front of any surname — you could even have von Schmidt! It does, however, mean that they may be listed in one of the various books on the German nobility. Incidentally the old nobility normally abbreviate "von" to "v". to differentiate themselves from "modern nobility".

The official status of the nobility in the German Empire was abolished in 1919 but the titles still continue in use. The main degrees of nobility were: König (King), Elector (a ruler with a vote in the election of the Holy Roman Emperor), Fürst (Prince), Grosherzog (Grand Duke), Herzog (Duke), Graf (Count or Earl), Freiherr (Baron) and Reichsritter (Imperial knight). From 1764 the "Gothaische Genealogische Hofkalendar" (or Gotha Genealogical Court Calendar) was published in German and French editions — it is better known in UK by its French title "Almanac de Gotha". These and other publications on the nobility ceased in 1942 and did not resume after the War though I see that the Almanac de Gotha has just started publishing again.[38]

In 1945 a foundation called "Deutsches Adelsarchiv" (or "German Archive of Nobility") was started at Marburg in Hesse. In 1951 publication started on the series called "Genealogisches Handbuch des Adels" of which 121 volumes had been published by 2000. A full set is on open access in the Humanities I Reading Room of the new British Library at St Pancras. While it is in German, it is set out much like the Burkes Peerage and is easy to understand. A comprehensive index to this series (and other publications) called "Stammfolgen-Verzeichnisse 1994" was published in 1994. The publishers, C A Starke Verlag of Limburg, have just (2000) brought out a full surname index to volumes 1 to 20 on CD-ROM and the Anglo German FHS has purchased a copy and is subscribing to the series.

In addition the same publishers publish a single alphabetic sequence of the nobility called "Adelslexikon" ("the Lexicon of the Nobility"). Seven volumes had been published up to 1996, the last volume covering Kre-Lod. It includes all proven noble families, except those extinct before 1800, and puts special emphasis on families ennobled after 1850. I do not know of any sets in UK and I have not heard anything of it after 1996.

Another useful source is "Deutsches Geschlechterbuch" ("The German Lineage Book") which began publication in 1889. This is more equivalent to the Landed Gentry and the volumes are often geographically-based ie there are 5 volumes for Baden, 1 for the Baltic States, 3 for Brandenburg, etc. By 1996 a total of 202 volumes had been published and these too are included in the index "Stammfolgen-Verzeichnisse 1994" referred to above.[39] However, a full surname index to volumes 1 to 209 has been published on CD-ROM and the publishers have just (2000) begun to publish back volumes on CD-ROM too (only volumes 1 to 10, on a single CD-ROM, are out yet). Again I do not know of any sets in the UK but the Anglo-German FHS is subscribing to the CD-ROM series.

Coats of Arms

The German for coats of arms is "Wappen". There are several publications that list and show German coats of arms, besides the Genealogical Dictionaries described above, and many claim a connection with a Johann Siebmacher of Nuremburg who died in 1611. He published a book of coats of arms, "Wappenbuch", in 1605 and there have been countless editions since then. Again there is an index that covers all of them: "General-Index zu den Siebmacherschen Wappenbüchern, 1605-1961" by Hanns Jäger-

Sunstenau, published by Akademische Druck und Verlagsanstalt, Graz, Austria, 1964. There is a set in the Rare Books reading room in the British Library.

Unlike English arms it appears that coats of arms can be borne undifferenced by several members of the family at the same time and the designs often seem (to English eyes) unusually pictorial. Also the blazon is commonly in plain German rather than the Norman-French we are used to.[40] If you cannot get your hands on one of these German publications, a useful source covering all Europe is Rietstap's Armorial. It lists the armorial families in alphabetical order and, in a separate volume, illustrates the arms.[41]

Auswanderer or German Emigrant records

In most German States an individual was not free to leave the State without permission. Before leaving they were supposed to seek leave in writing from the local ruler. Young men had to show that they had done their compulsory national service (generally between the ages of 17 and 21), that they were not leaving behind dependants (eg parents, wives, children) who might become chargeable to the State in the future, and that they had settled all their debts (and could prove it!). As you can imagine these applications could give rise to a lot of useful genealogical information. Many of these records have been indexed and the relevant archives may hold those indexes. In some cases, such as Württemburg, the indexes are being published.[42] If you know the State the immigrant came from, you could write to see if there is such an index. Most archives in Germany apear to have records of "Auswanderung" but they are not much use without an index unless you know where the emigrant came from.

Over the last few years the Land of Lower Saxony has been funding an index of all emigrants from the former States that now are part of their Land. Unfortunately, they decided to include only those emigrants who left Europe for America, Australia, etc.; it does not include those who just moved within Europe and so emigrants to UK are omitted. This is annoying but it might still be worth checking in the index as many emigrants possibly intended to go to America but got no further than England!

Of course, many could not meet the criteria to be allowed to leave, or did not think it worth risking being refused. They slipped away without asking. In many cases, however, there may well be indexes which include them too — when they failed to appear for their military service or it was otherwise noticed that they had left, their names were published in the local newspapers as deserters and these too may well have been indexed. Those who slipped away illegally and did not turn up to fulfil their military service will, in many cases, have forfeited their German State citizenship. This might explain the German people who claim to be of no citizenship when eg they naturalize.

German Passenger Lists

The most significant surviving sets of records of emigrants departing from Germany by ship are the Hamburg Passenger Lists. These cover passengers leaving Hamburg between 1850 and 1934 — nearly 6 million entries. The details from the original ships' lists include: age, occupation, marital status, city of origin, and the name of the ship and its destination and date of sailing. The LDS Church has microfilmed the Hamburg Lists and you can order the relevant film through your local LDS Library. You will need to consult their Family History Library Catalog to get the right reference. The lists for 1850-54 are in alphabetical order so there is no need for an index. After 1854 there are two main series with separate (usually annual) indexes: Direct Lists (where the ship went from Hamburg to America or elsewhere outside Europe without any intermediate stops) 1854-1934; and Indirect Lists (where the ship made an intermediate stop) 1854-1910. The latter lists are, of course, of more use to those looking for Germans in UK!

If you are unhappy with the idea of looking through records in German and in an unfamiliar script, there is an alternative. The Historic Emigration Office, Hamburg, was originally set up in 1984 by the Hamburg Tourist Board and at one time had a staff of 5 answering enquiries. However, in 1995 the office was closed. It was then agreed, as a private arrangement between a Ms Sroka, who worked there, and the Tourist Office, that she would be sponsored by them to provide the service. The Hamburg Tourist Office provides the office accommodation and pays the bills but no salary. She has to make that up from the research. She has access to the films of the passenger lists of ships leaving Hamburg. If you can provide the year the person emigrated, she can provide full details from the films. She provides all this on a stamped and sealed certificate. She charges US$75.00 or DM100.00 for the search and will only accept payment in those currencies. If you want to make use of the service you should write to:

Historic Emigration Office,
c/o Elizabeth Sroka,
Burchardstraße 14,
D-20095 Hamburg,
Germany

The main difficulty is first obtaining the year of emigration. If you do not have it, perhaps you can work out the date from another source.

Hamburg was one of the main ports for German emigration at this period, especially from north Germany, and many ships went from there to UK, to North America and even to Australasia. However, there were other emigration ports: Bremen in Germany; Ostend in Belgium; Rotterdam in the Netherlands; and Le Havre in France. For Le Havre, you should write to:

Monsieur le Directeur des Service dArchives,
Archives Departmentales de Seine Maritimes,
F-76000 Rouen,
FRANCE

In that case you should, of course, write in French. Bremen (whose records were destroyed by the German Government in 1907 and then by bombing in WWII) was one of the smaller ports for emigrants to UK so we may not have lost too much. NB there are published lists of emigrants from Bremen but note that these were compiled from US inward port records and so are unlikely to include passengers who disembarked in UK. If you believe that your immigrant ancestor came via other European ports, it is still worth checking there to see if you can find the records. I believe that some still exist for Ostend and Rotterdam.

PART II
Tracing German Ancestors in the German-speaking parts of Europe

In what follows, I try to give a helpful overview of the kind of records that are likely to be available in most areas that are, or were formerly, parts of Germany. I refer you to the Introduction for an explanation of the political and geographical problems. There are several publications available that give the addresses of archives, civil registration offices and Family History Societies and that go into more detail than is possible here about the local arrangements for consulting archives. [43]

German Historical Geography

As mentioned in the Introduction, Germany did not become a single state until 1871 (if then!). Before then there were many separate States and their names, boundaries and alliances changed frequently over the centuries. You cannot take a snapshot of the political situation at some time in the past and say that that is the "original" form. That is why you need good maps of the area you are interested in and an idea of the history of the area. There are some published books and articles in English but you may have to obtain a good German-language history of your area and translate it! Look out for old, pre-1914, school atlases which can often be found cheaply in second hand bookshops. You can do research in Germany without knowing any German but you will do much better if you can read and write a bit.[44]

Records Microfilmed by the LDS Church

If you cannot get to Germany very easily, do not fret. The LDS Church has been microfilming archives from the German-speaking parts of Europe for decades and there are vast collections of those microfilms in

Salt Lake City from where they can be ordered in the usual way. I wish that they would keep more of the German material in their UK Family History Libraries (FHLs) but, if more people here order German material, perhaps they will get the message. The microfilming does not just cover parish registers, though large numbers of them have been filmed, but police records, passenger lists, censuses, court records, land records and many printed books. The best place to start is the regularly up-dated Family History Library Catalog on CD-ROM which should be in all FHLs. In many cases below I draw attention to important documents that are available from FHLs but, just because I do not mention it, do not assume that the document has not been filmed. Check in the Catalog — and do it regularly as it is up-dated several times a year.[45]

The German Alphabet

This is as good a time as any to introduce one of the main difficulties involved in research in Germany: the alphabet. Before the end of the Second World War, German was written in a different alphabet. Many of you will be familiar with the printed "Gothic", "Fraktur" or "black letter" form. The equivalent handwritten form is, alas, equally difficult to read until you become used to it. But do not let me put you off. It is no different from learning to read eg English 17th century handwriting and the technique for learning it is much the same: practice, practice and more practice! There is a useful bilingual book published in Germany called: "The German Script". Many also swear by a book by an American lady, Edna M. Bentz, on how to read it and anyone seriously intending to do research in German records before 1945 should get a copy of one or the other.[46] As a general rule, however, Roman Catholic records are written in Latin in italic script which is similar to the alphabet that we use; such records are therefore much easier to use (so long as Latin is not a problem for you!).

Civil Registration

Civil Registration did not cover the whole of the then German Empire until 1876. Even then the records are not kept centrally but are usually in the local civil registry office: the "Standesamt" of the area; often this is physically in the Town Hall or "Rathaus". For some parts of Germany, civil registration started earlier: Prussia and most of the Eastern provinces started in 1874; some former states that were conquered by the French during the Revolutionary and Napoleonic Wars, like Alsace-Lorraine (Elsass-Lothringen), the Rhineland, the Palatinate (Pfalz) and Baden, started in 1792; Westphalia began in 1808; Hanover in 1809; and Bremen and Oldenburg in 1811. Once you know the area that your ancestor came from, you need to do some further research to find out when civil registration started locally. The map on pages 54 and 55 gives you an outline to start from.

To obtain birth, marriage or death certificates, therefore, you need to know where and roughly when the event took place. If you know, you should write (preferably in German) to:

Standesamt,
D-[plus post code], [name of the town],
Germany

If the event took place in a small village, you will need to find the appropriate Standesamt by using a Gazetteer.[47] In a large city like Berlin or Hamburg there are likely to be several Standesamts and you will need to find the right one if you can. It is usually best to find the address of the City Rathaus and use the same postal code. If you do not write German, there are a number of publications which give draft letters in German so that you only need to fill in the blanks with names and dates![48] Dont forget though that you will still have to be able to read the reply when it arrives.

Postcodes are particularly important when you write to Germany. When you write from outside Germany they should always be prefixed with "D-". The postcode itself, a 5 digit number, can be obtained from a publication called: "Postleitzahlenbuch" (or Postcode book). NB the postcodes changed in 1993 so do not use any postcodes from before that date.

The Civil Registration records in Germany are not always as accessible to the public as the British equivalents are. Indeed, there is effectively a 100-year (and more!) rule in operation whereby you need to demonstrate that you are a descendant of the individual concerned before you will be allowed to have the details from the records. I understand, however, that it is largely up to the official at the Standesamt how strictly this is applied. It is clearly only going to be a problem for events in the last century or so and I suggest that you apply in the usual way and see what happens. As you are ordering the record because you believe you are a relative, the Standesamt may well be willing to give you the benefit of the doubt, but don't count on it. An assertion that you are a direct descendant of the person whose certificate you are ordering, and a draft family tree showing the relationship, should be adequate.

If you are having difficulty in obtaining a certificate, you may decide to look for the church registration of baptism, marriage or burial instead (see below). The churches may be less likely to consider themselves to be covered by the privacy laws.

You should not send money with your first letter but explain that you want to impose a ceiling on the amount of money you wish to spend. The Standesamt will let you know in their reply how much it will cost and you can obtain a cheque in marks or euros from your local bank. There may also be a preliminary search fee of about 9 marks; the Standesamt will tell you. They will often accept this in German stamps (Briefmarken) which can be cheaper to obtain than a bank draft!

The information you get on Civil Registration certificates varies from State to State and from time to time but, generally speaking, you get more useful data than you get in the equivalent English, Welsh or Irish certificate. It also has the advantage over the church registers that, as the form itself is printed, it is easier to read.

Church Registers

Once you have got back before Civil Registration, or if you cannot obtain the certificate, the next major source is the "Kirchenbücher", church books or registers. As a general rule, they start in the 16th or 17th centuries and continue through to the present day. Also they contain considerably more information that you could hope to find in the equivalent British registers.[49] There were three main Christian denominations in the German-speaking areas: the Roman Catholic, the Lutheran or Evangelical and the Reformed Lutheran or Calvinist churches. Each kept registers and they are held either in the parish, in the Town or City Archives (Stadtarchiv), State Archives (Staatarchiv) or have been gathered together into special church archives. For detailed lists and addresses consult books like the Anglo-German FHS's "Useful Addresses for German Research" and "The German Research Companion".

38

The main types of German Church records of use to family historians are:

Baptisms — *Taufregister*: The entries normally provide the child's date and place of baptism, date of birth, mother's name, name, residence and occupation of father, name and occupation of mother's father, names and residences of witnesses or godparents. Many provide even more useful information.

Confirmations — *Konfirmation*: Children in the Roman Catholic and Protestant churches were usually confirmed between 11 and 16 years of age. These registers are more common in Germany than in England and can often provide additional information about the family a decade or so after the birth.

Marriage — *Trauregister*: These normally give the date & place of the marriage, name, age, residence & occupation of the groom, the name & age of the bride, the names of bride's and groom's parents, their residences and (the fathers') occupations, the name of the previous spouse if either party was widowed, and the names, residences & occupations of the witnesses.

Death — *Sterberegister*: These usually give the name, occupation, age at death, date & place of death and of burial, and the names of surviving spouse and children. Sometimes the cause of death is also given.

Burial — *Begräbnisse*: These normally give the name of the deceased, their age at death, residence, occupation, dates and places of death and burial, cause of death and the names of any surviving spouse. Sometimes the gravestone inscription is also given — very useful where, as is usually the case in Germany, the grave plots are cleared and re-used every 30 years or so.

Deutsche Zentralstelle für Genealogie (German Central Office for Genealogy)

In Leipzig is the German national genealogy collection. They have been collecting materials on genealogy since the beginning of the 20th century and one of their main sources is a slip index (the "ASTAKA" or "Ahnenstammkartei") of over 1 million slips which indexes manuscript and printed family histories (including articles in books and magazines) in their collection. It is well worth a search, just in case your family has already been researched. The LDS Church has microfilmed the slip index but the organisation of the slips is so complex that you need a book to discover which film to order.[51] You can write to the DZfG in English to ask if your German family is covered but, if you want a speedy reply, it would be best to write in German. Their reply will be in German. This will only work if the surname is uncommon in Germany or you know in which town or village in Germany the family were living. They will not charge for answering your first enquiry but thereafter charge 70 DM an hour and 1 DM for an A4 photocopy (as at mid 1998). However as they have access to the slip index and know how to use it, the time taken in a search should not be long.

They also hold the copies of German parish registers made from 1935 to 1945 as part of the German Government's policy of preserving genealogical material by the Reichsippenamt. They have published 3 volumes listing the registers and these are available for sale at the DZfG office (the Anglo-German FHS also has a set). If you discover that they hold a register of relevance to your research, you could ask them to research in it for you. However, the LDS Church has copied all of those registers and you would be able to order the microfilm through them in the normal way (if you feel able to deal with the handwriting!). The other main source they hold is a virtually complete set of Ortssippenbücher (see below) and asking them to look for you is often the quickest way to see if your ancestral parishes are covered.

Their address is

> **Deutsche Zentralstelle für Genealogie.**
> **Schongauerstrasse 1,**
> **D-04329 Leipzig,**
> **Germany**

Wills

As in UK, wills (Testamente or Testamentsakten) can be a fruitful genealogical source if you can only find them. The best place to look is the local Amtsgerichte or Courthouse. The records will be in German and handwritten so it will take some effort to find and read your ancestors will. But it will be worth the effort.

Censuses

There were no censuses (Volkszählungen) covering the whole of the German Empire until 1871. There were, however, many more localised ones taken by particular States for various reasons as far back as the 17th century. Where censuses were taken, as nowadays, for statistical purposes, the statistics were centralised, but the census returns, where they survive, should be in the local archives. There was a particularly useful census for the Grand Duchy of Mecklenburg-Schwerin in 1819: for each individual in the State it gives the name, sex, religion, date and place of birth, spouse's name and occupation, how long the individual had been living in the current parish, where and when the spouse was born and how long resident in the current parish. It has been indexed by the Immigrant Genealogical Society and they will undertake a search and let you have the details transcribed and translated into English for a small fee![52, 53] The census (but not the index) is available on microfilm through the LDS library. Schleswig-Holstein is another part of Germany that has good early census records[54] and it is well worth looking for one in your own area of interest.

Military and Naval Records[55]

First the bad news: the records of the Prussian Army, the German Army from 1871 and the records of most of the other German States Armies after about 1867 were destroyed by fire at Potsdam in the Battle for Berlin in 1945. Virtually none of the records survived. However, those military archives that do survive are kept at the Bundesarchiv in Freiburg im Breisgau in Baden-Württemburg:

> **Abt MA des Bundesarchiv,**
> **Wiesenthalstraße 10,**
> **D-79115 Freiburg im Breisgau,**
> **GERMANY**

The German equivalent of the Commonwealth War Graves Commission, the Volksbund Deutsche Kreigsgraberfursorge e.V, has set up a searchable database on the Internet at www.Volksbund.de which would be worth searching if you think a relative may have been killed in action.

Some German States army records do survive. The Bavarian Army records up to 1919 are complete and are kept in the War Archive in

41

Munich. The records of the armies of other German States, like Baden, Brunswick, Hanover, Hesse, Mecklenburg and Württemberg, before 1867 (in a few cases, 1871) are kept in the individual States archives.

Army records, where they survive, can be very helpful as most young men had to undertake military service. It is also worth noting that there were several wars involving Germans in the mid 19th century, "the Wars of Unification", which make it even more likely that your ancestor will appear in the records. To find him, though, you need to know the Army, the Regiment and the Company! This is not necessarily as difficult as it sounds as many parishes and towns had their own lists of the young men liable to military service saying what happened to them; these can serve a different function as many emigrated to avoid military service and the lists may say "nach Amerika" or "nach England". Each town was associated with a specific Regiment and, using gazetteers, it should be relatively easy to find which one.

A useful source, particularly for Prussia where the other records are lost, could be the Military Church Books:[56] each Army chaplain in the Prussian Army, and in many other German State's Armies, had his own baptism, marriage and burial registers and these often survive. They are clearly only likely to record your ancestor if he married, had children baptised or was buried during his time with the army but they can be very helpful where, as with Prussia, the Army records themselves do not survive..

Records of officers are easier to find as there are several equivalents to the British "Army List" known as "Ranglisten". Each State that had its own army is likely to have published a regular listing of the officers.[57] Of course, where the archives were not destroyed in 1945 there will be manuscript records too.

Other useful publications that can substitute for the lost archives are the casualty lists. These are available for every German war since 1866 and list, by Regiment, all those wounded or killed and give their places of origin and, sometimes, their dates of birth. These are printed volumes and should appear in German libraries as well as the Bundesarchiv in Freiburg im Breisgau.

German Navy records appear to have been kept with the Army records and so those for Prussia and for Germany after 1867 will have been destroyed in 1945. There were, however, Naval Churchbooks on the same lines as Army Churchbooks and these can be looked for in the same way. Where a German State before 1867 had its own navy, the records will probably be with the army records.

Registration with the Police

Germany has always kept more detailed records of its inhabitants than the UK and the results can be particularly helpful for the genealogist. From about 1830 (in some places, earlier) the police kept detailed records of all residents in their district. The records were kept in the "Einwohnermeldeamt" or Residents Registration Office. Every person was registered with details of where they came from and where they went, their relations and any remarks the police recorded. The amount of information is amazing including every address they lived at in the district covered, with the dates. As you might expect, the more recent information is usually closed, probably for 100 years, but, for periods before 1890 it is well worth tracking them down. Even for later periods it is worth trying, just in case. If not in the existing Einwohnermeldeamt for the district, the older records may well have found their way into the Stadtarchiv or Staatarchiv.

Similar records are called "Melderegister. In Leipzig, for example, the Einwohnermelde- register covers 1811 to 1893 and the Melderegister covers 1890 to 1949. Both have been microfilmed by the LDS Church and are available on microfilm at the LDS libraries.[58]

Of particular importance for immigrants to Britain who travelled via Hamburg are the equivalent Hamburg police records.[59] They are kept at the Hamburg Staatsarchiv but those for 1834 to 1929 have been microfilmed by the LDS Church and are available through their libraries. These records can be used to supplement the Hamburg Passenger Lists (see pages 33-34) which may give the passenger's last place of residence, frequently "Hamburg", as his or her address. The police records should give his or her date and place of birth among other vital information. The same Department dealt with the issue of Passports and the records from 1851 to 1929 are also available. NB that passports could be issued to people who were not citizens of Hamburg, especially if they were temporary residents who wanted to go abroad but could not get back to their home State to get a passport.

Dorfsippenbücher, Ortssippenbücher and Ortsfamilienbücher

In the 1930s an organisation, the Reichssippenamt, was set up in Germany with the aim of indexing all the German parish registers and reconstituting the family trees of the families therein. By the outbreak of the Second World War only 30 parishes had been published. These were the "Dorfsippenbücher" or "village family books". The books do not just provide an index but link each individual to his or her family and the generations before and following. These were by no means the first such publications some of which date from the 19th century. After WWII, publishing started again in the 1950s and the books were now called "Ortssippenbücher" or "Ortsfamilienbücher". Several of the volumes cover towns that are no longer part of Germany eg the Banat now in Northern Serbia. The German Central Office for Genealogy in Leipzig (Deutsche Zentralstelle für Genealogie) (see pages 39-40) holds a virtually complete set of these books and I understand that about 200 new volumes are published each year and are added to their collection. The LDS Library in Salt Lake City also has a large number of them.[60]

Besides the parish registers themselves, the editors of these books often made use of other archive sources in identifying the individuals eg tax lists, emigration records, censuses, etc. It is therefore always worth checking whether the town or village you are interested in has been covered by one of these Sippenbücher. I understand that even a large City like Leipzig has been covered! Recently published Ortssippenbücher may still be available to purchase from the publishers; it is worth asking the Deutsche Zentralstelle if you write to them; many are published by the local German family history societies.

Family Registers in the Kingdom of Württemberg

To illustrate the possibilities of finding useful records in different States, there are the Familienregistern (Family Registers) of the Kingdom of Württemberg (within its 1806 borders). The registers were the result of a Government decree but were actually kept by the parish priest or parson. Each family has a separate page or pages and entries contain the name of the head of household, his date & place of birth (ie not baptism though that might also be included), social standing, profession, residence, date & place of marriage and of death; similar details for the spouse, his and her parents and his children. All entries are cross-referenced to other families in the parish where necessary. All registers are fully indexed and all parishes are covered from 1815 onwards (so, with living people being covered, the entries could go back to the mid 18th century!). Unfortunately the German privacy laws mean that the information after 1900 may not be available (but it is worth asking!). The LDS Church has microfilmed nearly all the records which are listed under "church records" in their Catalog and so can be ordered in the usual way. The original records are usually still in the parish with the churchbooks.

Burger Lists or Books and Trade Directories
Another source that can enable you to place your ancestor in a specific town and time are burger lists or books. These are roughly equivalent to English Guild or Freemen's records and survive for many German cities and towns up to the mid 19th century.[61] The books often provide useful information like occupation, address and date and place of birth. Many have been published and the LDS Library in Salt Lake City also has a large number of them. An "Addreßbuch", equivalent to a British "trade directory", will often be available for most large German cities or towns from the late 18th century onwards. As in UK, the later editions often contain more detail that the earlier ones. As to availability, the most likely place to find one would be in the city or town itself.

The former German territories in Eastern Europe
A major problem with German research that British researchers are not likely to have experienced before, is the effect of significant changes in the boundaries of the Countries concerned over the years and particularly over the last 50 years! Few countries have experienced such a number of major changes in jurisdiction and those changes are likely to have affected where the records are now to be found. This is an especial problem in the lands east of the current German border that had been German, or subject to the Prussian Crown, for centuries. Many of those lands are now in Poland, the Ukraine, Lithuania and even Russia (eg Kaliningrad formerly Königsberg).

There is no easy way of finding out where the records of individual cities, towns or parishes now are. It is not even easy to find out where the places are now — so many have changed their names. The easiest way to find the place is to look in a contemporary map or atlas for the name you know and then compare it with a modern map of the area to see what it is called now. The Anglo-German FHS keeps useful sets of 19th and 20th century maps and offers this service to its members. Some of the name changes are relatively easy (like Danzig to Gdansk and Stettin to Szczecin) but some names have changed completely (like Bromberg to Bydgoszcz and Memel to Klaipeda).[62]

Once you have identified the place, you need to find out where the records are now kept. For example, many of the civil registration records for places that were in the German Empire from 1871 to 1945, but are now no longer in Germany, are still in the town of origin. Equally, however, many were brought west by refugees at the end of the Second World War and are now in Standesamt I in Berlin. Also many German church registers, etc. were brought back into what is now Germany at the end of the War. Evangelical (Lutheran) records may be in their archives in Berlin at:

Evangelisches Zentralarchiv in Berlin,
Jebenstraße 3,
D-10623 Berlin,
GERMANY

Roman Catholic records may be at:

Bischöfliches Zentralarchiv Regensburg,
St-Peters-Weg 11-13,
D-93047 Regensburg,
GERMANY

A useful source of information on places in the former Eastern Territories is the Prussian Privy Archive in Berlin:

Geheimes Staatsarchiv Preußicher Kulturbesitz,
Archivstraße 12-14,
D-14195 Berlin (Dahlem),
GERMANY

which holds many records relating to the German population in former parts of Prussia. For example they hold the main State archives of Königsberg (now Kaliningrad, a Russian enclave on the Baltic) which had been held in the archives at Göttingen from 1953 to 1978. I understand that they are very helpful in replying to postal enquiries.

Records that have recently become available for research can be very helpful in tracing people who came into Germany from the former eastern territories and the German settlements in Central, East and South East Europe, and even tracing refugees of German origin from France, Belgium, etc. during the Second World War. From 1939 to 1945 over 2.1 million people from those areas emigrated to Germany. They were required to complete pedigree charts and family group records showing documented births, marriages and deaths for each individual, their parents and their children. They were processed by the Einwandererzentralstelle (EWZ) and the indexed records generated have been microfilmed and are available at the Bundesarchiv in Berlin at:

> **Abt R des Bundesarchiv,**
> **Fickensteinallee 63,**
> **Postfach 450 569,**
> **D-12175 Berlin,**
> **GERMANY**

They were formerly in the Berlin Document Centre.[63]

Also transferred from the Berlin Document Centre to the Bundesarchiv in Berlin (same address as above) were the records of the Nazi party 1933-45 which contain membership files for Nazi organisations and applications for Party membership. I understand that they are well-indexed. Another part of the Bundesarchiv holds the records relating to compensation claims by Germans displaced by the Second World War and its aftermath:

> **Abt LS des Bundesarchiv,**
> **Justus-Liebig-Straße 8A,**
> **D-95447 Bayreuth,**
> **GERMANY**

If the place you are interested in is now in Poland, you can start by writing to the Polish Regional Archives covering the place; you should first have ascertained where it is and its Polish name.[64] You may get away with writing in English though Polish is recommended; they will reply in Polish!

Parish records are much more likely to be scattered: in Poland, for example, the religion of the Poles was Roman Catholicism whereas most of the Germans there were Lutherans or Calvinists. The Roman Catholic records are usually with the churches or the Diocese but many of the Protestant records have been moved back to Germany. For example, the Deutsche Zentralstelle für Genealogie ("German Central Office for Genealogy) in Leipzig (see pages 39-40) holds large numbers of copies of the registers for the eastern provinces of Posen, East and West Prussia, Pomerania and Silesia, and for other former German-speaking territories like Bessarabia and Bukovina (in Roumania), the Baltic States, Sudetenland (in the Czech Republic), Slovenia and the South Tyrol.

The LDS church has also been microfilming large numbers of registers in Eastern Europe and the microfilms can be borrowed in the usual way from FHLs. The *"Genealogical Guide"*,[65] contain lists of addresses of the local and national archives, and of societies for those people who left the former German territories after the Second World War, and details of many other useful sources.

The Austro-Hungarian Empire

Lands that had significant German-speaking populations and that were formerly part of the Austro-Hungarian Empire are also affected: the Czech Republic, Slovakia, Hungary, the Italian and Austrian Tyrol, Roumania, and Serbia and most of the other successor states of Yugoslavia. The problems and solutions are much the same as for the former German Eastern Provinces. In the Austro-Hungarian Empire there was no civil registration as such. Up to 1781, the local Roman Catholic priest was expected to include in his parish registers details of everyone in the parish whatever their religion: whether Catholic, Protestant, Jewish, Muslim or of no religion. If you are lucky there may also survive a parish "Status Animarum" ("Condition of the Souls") which lists everyone in the parish with details of their family, religion, morals, etc. The Jewish community were allowed to keep their own records after 1781 but Protestants not until 1849. Civil registration in Austria itself started as late as 1939.

Vienna

As an example of some other records that might survive, let us take the City of Vienna. Useful sources are: Einwohnermeldezettel ("population register cards") 1850-1920 which are arranged alphabetically with males first followed by females; Einwohnerkartei ("population registers") 1700-1950 also arranged alphabetically; indexes to Vienna wills (Testaments) 1548-1850 and estates (Verlaßenschaften) 1789-1850; passport registers (Paßregister) 1792-1918, workers' registers (Arbeiterprotokolle) 1860-1919, Nazi pedigree documentation (Abstammungsnachweise) 1938-45, all of which are indexed.[66]

There are also military personnel files (Grundbuchblätter) 1780-1930 for soldiers born in the City of Vienna, arranged alphabetically. Incidentally those military personnel files should survive for all the former parts of the Austro-Hungarian Empire. They were held alphabetically by province and those relating to former provinces that are no longer part of Austria may have been sent to the archives of the successor states eg those for Hungary should be in Budapest. The difficulty arises when the former province has been split between Countries. It is best to start by writing to the War Archives in Vienna at:

Osterreichisches Staatsarchiv,
Kreigsarchiv,
Nottendorfergasse 2,
A-1030 Wien,
AUSTRIA

All the above records for Vienna, and many others, have been microfilmed by the LDS church and should be available through their local Libraries.

Hungary

In Hungary, civil registration started on 1st October 1895 and the records are kept in the local town halls though the National Archives has duplicates and will undertake a search for you. You should write, in Hungarian, German or English to:

Magyar Orszagos Leveltar,
Becsikapu ter 4, Postafiok 3,
H-1250 Budapest 1,
HUNGARY

Hungary is much smaller now than it was from 1895 to 1919 and many of the former Hungarian areas are now in surrounding countries like Slovenia, Croatia, Serbia (especially the Vojvoidina), the Czech Republic,

Slovakia, Roumania and the Ukraine. On the other hand, the archives of the Austro-Hungarian State before 1919 are likely to be useful for records such as censuses and Army and Navy records. Once again, one of the US-published books on Germanic research, with their lists of addresses, maps, etc., is essential to a serious researcher.[67] To do research in the area of the Austro-Hungarian Empire during the last 100 years or so, you really need a good history of the area and a good set of maps!

Switzerland
Swiss citizens gain their citizenship from their family's home town or village and, even if an individual has moved away, their birth, marriage and death details are still sent back to the home town and recorded there – even from another Country. You therefore need to know the family's home town or village. Civil registration did not start until 1st January 1876 but the parish registers can go back to the 16th century and are often found in the same office. In many cases full genealogies have been compiled by the local authorities – some of which employ a full-time genealogist! [68]

Denmark
The present German Land of Schleswig-Holstein was ruled by the King of Denmark until it was conquered by Prussia in 1864. Germany also included North Schleswig from 1864 until it was returned to Denmark in 1920. Altona, which is now a suburb of Hamburg, was a Danish port until 1864! If your researches take you back to this area before the 1860s, you will need to use the Danish archives some of which are held locally but some are in eg Copenhagen. Civil registration in Denmark did not start until 1874 but the church records are good and should still be held locally as in Germany. Surnames can be a problem as the patronymic system (being named after the father without a true surname) often continued in rural areas until the mid 19th century.[69]

Heligoland
The island of Heligoland (Helgoland in German) in the North Sea opposite Hamburg, was ruled by Denmark until it was captured by the Royal Navy during the Napoleonic Wars. It was ruled as a British Colony from 1807 until 1890 when it was ceded to Germany in exchange for Zanzibar and

other African territories. The inhabitants (about 2,000) were engaged in fishing and piloting ships in the North Sea. In the 1850s German recruits for the German-British Legion (see page 21) were registered there and then shipped to England for training. The island was evacuated and heavily bombed after the First and Second World Wars. Most surviving records are held locally: the churchbooks are at:

> **Kirchenkreis Süderdithmarschen,**
> **Kampstraße 8a,**
> **D-25704 Meldorf,**
> **GERMANY**

and the local civil registration records from 1875 (even though it was still a British Colony at the time) are held at:

> **Gemeinde Helgoland,**
> **Gemeinderverwaltung,**
> **D-27498 Helgoland,**
> **GERMANY.**

There are some records in the PRO including the 1881 census for the island.[70] It has been suggested that there is a copy of the 1851 census somewhere in England too and I would be very interested if anyone can find it.

German Genealogical Societies

As in UK there are several family history societies in Germany. Their journals are, however, in German and it is probably not worth joining unless you have some German. The Societies are usually geographically based but cover wider areas than the equivalent societies in England. For example the Family History and Heraldry Society of Württemberg and Baden covers the whole Land of Baden-Württemberg and its magazine is called the "Südwest-deutsche Blätter für Familien- und Wappenkunde" (the South West German Newspaper for Family History and Heraldry). To find the most up-to-date listing of the societies and their addresses, you should look in one of the several books already mentioned that give useful German addresses.[71] It is worth noting that several societies have a policy of publishing registers and other records for their area and it might be worth joining for a year or so to see what is available; prices are often cheaper to members.

There is also a quarterly general publication for family history queries that covers the whole of Germany and appears to be distributed with all German family history society magazines: it is called *"Familienkundliche Nachrichten*. It is published by Verlag Degener AG, Postfach 1360, D-91403, Neustadt a.d. Aisch, Germany. Requests for genealogical information can be inserted in it free by members of German Family History Societies; if you are not a member you can write to the publishers to insert a query. The queries are in German but are very similar in form and content to Members Queries in British Family History Society magazines. You can send your enquiry in English and the publishers will translate it into an appropriate German form. They will bill you before the enquiry appears but the cost is quite reasonable.

Some Internet Sites

As the sites available on the Internet are so many and varied and can change in content, nature and address from time to time, I do not intend to try to give a comprehensive listing here. Instead, I will give some of the more important sites for German genealogy, all of which provide links to other useful sites.

The Federation of Eastern European Family History Societies site *feefhs.org* contains the web sites of all its nearly 200 member societies. The Federation's policy is to ensure that each of the existing Countries in East and Central Europe has a society catering to those interested in its genealogy. This is already largely the case and, as the Federation is based in USA, most of the societies are US-based and conduct their affairs in English! Besides the details of the societies, this web site also holds detailed historical maps of East and Central Europe (including Germany) and some large databases that can be searched on line.

For example there is a full name index to the 1835, 1845 and 1855 censuses for Ranzau in Schleswig-Holstein; an index, "Die Vorfahren", to all the 114,000 surnames appearing in all 21 volumes of the late Myron Gruenwald's newsletter on Pomeranian research: **"Die Pommerschen Leute"**; and many miscellaneous smaller indices. There is an on-line facility at the web site enabling you to have all these indices checked in a single search for your surname.

Another "gateway" site is that of the "German Genealogy Home Page" at *www.genealogy.net/gene* It is German-based but, in most cases, provides a choice of getting the pages in German or English. A particularly useful section is that called "Regional Resources", which provides historical, geographical and research background on most of the German-speaking (or former German-speaking) parts of Europe, indexed by the names of the States or former States. For example, under Baden-Württemberg there are links to: General Information; Associations and Societies; Genealogical and Historical Records; Gazetteers and Maps; Bibliography and Literature; Archives and Libraries; Miscellaneous; and Other Internet Resources. In addition there are sections on "Beginners Tips" and "Frequently Asked Questions" (FAQs). It also provides translation services by e-mail, a facility to identify German placenames, draft letters in German to churches, archives, etc and some on-line databases. Overall this site is a source of information equivalent to the British Genuki site.

The international pages at *www.rootsweb.com* are another useful source of information on research in the various parts of Germany. This is a US-based site and the pages are all in English.

Overall Cyndis List at *www.cyndislist.com* is still the best place to start from with over 93,800 links to other genealogical sites; all well organised so that you can easily find the sites that interest you.

The Internet is growing all the time and is well worth "surfing". If you have not already tried it, why not type your German surname into a search engine and see what turns up? You may be surprised.

START OF CIVIL REGISTRATION IN GERMANY

Map of German Empire 1871-1919 showing start dates of Civil Registration.

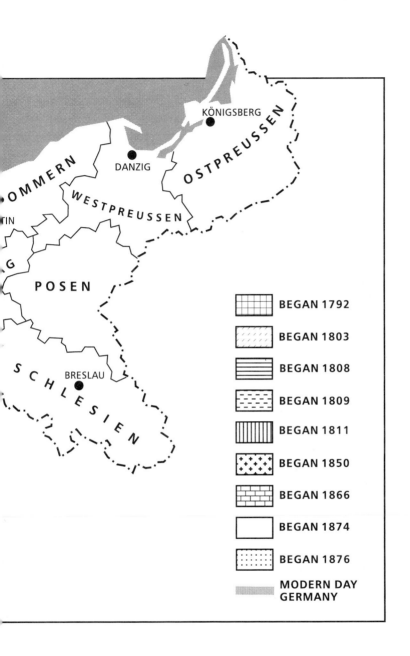

KÖNIGSBERG

DANZIG

OSTPREUSSEN

POMMERN

WESTPREUSSEN

TIN

G

POSEN

SCHLESIEN

BRESLAU

	BEGAN 1792
	BEGAN 1803
	BEGAN 1808
	BEGAN 1809
	BEGAN 1811
	BEGAN 1850
	BEGAN 1866
	BEGAN 1874
	BEGAN 1876
	MODERN DAY GERMANY

PART III

Notes and Bibliography

1. *Germans in Britain since, 1500,* ed. by Panikos Panayi, pub. The Hambledon Press, London, 1996, and: *German Immigrants in Britain during the Nineteenth Century, 1815-1914,* by Panikos Panayi, pub. Berg, Oxford, 1995.

2. *Little Germany. Exile and Asylum in Victorian England,* by Rosemary Ashton, OUP, 1986, which looks at the experiences of the 1848 refugees in England.

3. *Immigrants and Aliens: A guide to sources on UK immigration and citizenship,* by Roger Kershaw and Mark Pearsall, Public Record Office Readers' Guide no. 22, PRO, 2000.

4. *6. How to find and use Denization and Naturalization Records after 1800,* PRO, Kew. Gives detailed instructions on how to obtain the papers from the Home Office file as well as the Certificate. NB this is not one of the leaflets in the pigeon holes in the Lobby but can only be obtained from behind the desk. You also have to call personally at the PRO to get a copy; they will not send you a copy in response to a postal request.

5. *Letters of Denization and Acts of Naturalization for Aliens in England, 1509-1603,* ed. William Page, pub. Huguenot Society of London, Quarto Series, vol. 8, 1893. *Letters of Denization and Acts of Naturalization for Aliens in England and Ireland, 1603-1700,* ed. William A Shaw, pub. Huguenot Society of London, Quarto Series, vol. 18, 1911. *Letters of Denization and Acts of Naturalization for Aliens in England and Ireland, 1701-1800,* ed. William A Shaw, pub. Huguenot Society of London, Quarto Series, vol. 27, 1923. These list all aliens whatever their origin and are not confined to those of French or Huguenot descent. The records to which they relate are usually at the PRO in Kew but the detailed introductions to the earlier volumes should be read to get the most from the records.

6. *The Plymouth Aliens List 1798 and 1803,* by V D Lipman in Miscellanies Part VI, The Jewish Historical Society of England, 1962, pp. 187-194.

7. The most comprehensive listing of information on these churches and their records is *The Records of German Churches of the British Isles 1550-1900, and other related records,* Research Guide Twelve, ed. by Pam Freeman and pub. Anglo-German FHS, 2000.

8. There is a history of the church in German and English *300 Years of St Mary's German Lutheran Church in London, 1694-1994,* by Suzanne Steinmetz, published in 1994 by the church at 10 Sandwich Street, London, WC1H 9PL.

9. *St George's German Lutheran Church, Alie Street, Aldgate, London. Marriages 1825-1896,* Record Series One, Anglo-German FHS, 1997. *St George's German Lutheran Church, Alie Street, Aldgate, London. Baptisms 1763-1895 and Burials 1818-53,* Record Series Two, Anglo-German FHS, 1997.

10. *St Paul's German Reformed Church, London. Baptisms 1824-1940, Marriages 1858-1938 and Burials 1832-1940,* Record Series Three, Anglo-German FHS, 1997.

11. *300 Years of the German Reformed Church in London,* by Rudolf Muhs. *Mitteilungsblatt,* Anglo-German FHS magazine, no. 42, Sept. 1997, pp 15-17.

12. *Memorials of St James's Palace,* by Edgar Shepherd, London, Longmans, Green and Co., 1894. 2 vols. vol. II, pp. 245-260, contains the most detailed history of the German Lutheran Royal Chapel to date.

13. *Germans at Coniston in the Seventeenth Century,* by W G Collingwood, MA, FSA, in *Transactions of the Cumberland & Westmorland Antiquarian & Archaeological Society,* vol. X, New Series, pp. 369-394. 1910. Contains detailed list of the Germans that appear in the parish registers of Crosthwaite and Coniston. See also: *Elizabethan Keswick. Extracts from the Original Account Books, 1564-1577, of the German Miners in the Archives of Augsburg,* by W G Collingwood, pub. 1912; reprinted, 1987, by Michael Moon's Bookshop, 41, 42 & 43 Roper Street, Whitehaven, Cumbria.

14. *The Shotley Bridge Swordmakers - Their Strange History,* by David Richardson, Northern History Booklet no. 37. pub. Frank Graham, 6 Queen's Terrace, Newcastle upon Tyne, NE2 2PL, 1973.

15. eg. *The Hull German Lutheran Church 1848-1998,* by Barbara M Robinson, pub. Highgate Publications (Beverley) Ltd. 4 Newbegin, Beverley, HU17 8EG.
16. **The Lutheran Church in Ireland, 1697-1997,** pub. Monika McCurdy & Alan Murphy for the Evangelisch-Lutherische Kirche in Irland, Lutherhaus, 24 Adelaide Road, Dublin, Belfast, 1997.
17. The Jewish Genealogical Society of Great Britain (JGSGB) is producing a very useful series of booklets including *Jewish Ancestors? A Beginner's Guide to Jewish Genealogy in Great Britain,* ed. by Rosemary Wenzerul, JGSGB, 2000, and *Jewish Ancestors? A Guide to Jewish Genealogy in Germany and Austria,* ed. by Thea Skyte, Randol Schoenberg & Rosemary Wenzerul, JGSGB, 2001. The older publication by the Society of Genealogists: **My** *Ancestor was Jewish: How can I find out more about him?* ed. by Michael Gandy, pub. in 1982, is still useful as is the more detailed section on Jewish research by Edgar R Samuel in *Sources for Roman Catholic and Jewish Genealogy and Family History,* by Don Steel, *National Index of Parish Registers* vol. 3, pub. Phillimore & Co, Chichester, 1974. The JGSGB also about to published *Jewish Genealogy? A Guide to Jewish Genealogy in Latvia and Estonia,* in March 2001 and we can look forward to others in the series. If you are interested in research in Jewish immigrants from Germany and elsewhere in Europe you really should join the JGSGB which publishes an excellent quarterly magazine *Shemot,* in English, and has a very useful website at **www.jgsgb.ort.org.**
18. See *Foreign Regiments in the British Army 1793-1802,* by C T Atkinson, Journal of the Society for Army Historical Research, vols. XXI-XXII (1942-1944); *The Auxiliaries: Foreign and Miscellaneous Regiments in the British Army 1802-1817,* by R L Yaple, Journal of the Society for Army Historical Research, vol. L (1972). Those articles provide potted histories of all the Regiments concerned and provide pointers on which had large German contingents.
19. The main book on the KGL is *History of the King's German Legion,* by N Ludlow Beamish, FRS, 2 vols, 1832-37, reprinted by Naval & Military Press, Dallington, East Sussex, 1997. In December 2000 the Anglo-German FHS published a much cheaper, useful and

well illustrated book on *The King's German Legion: Records and Research,* ed. by Gwen Davis.

20. There are a series of published volumes indexing the records in Hanover: *Garrisons Hannover,* ed by the late Jurgen Ritter for the Lower Saxony Family History Society in Germany. The Anglo-German FHS has a set.

21. The *German Regiments of the British Army,* Research Guide Seven, pub. Anglo-German FHS, March 1992.

22. *Naval Records for Genealogists,* by N A M Rodgers, PRO Handbooks no. 22, PRO 1998, is the best book on the records of the Royal Navy. On the Royal Marines the best book *is: Records of the Royal Marines,* by Garth Thomas, PRO Readers Guide no. 10, HMSO, 1994.

23. *Records of Merchant Shipping and Seamen,* by Kelvin Smith, Christopher T Watts & Michael J Watts, PRO Readers' Guide no. 20, was published in 1998 and is very useful for the records in the PRO. However, the best overall guide to the records of merchant seamen is *My Ancestor was a Merchant Seaman. How can I find out more about him?* by Christopher T and Michael J Watts, pub. Society of Genealogists in 1991, which covers records in other archives like those in the Guildhall Library. In practice, you need both.

24. *India Office Library and Records. A Brief Guide to Biographical Sources* by Ian A. Baxter, pub. British Library, 2nd ed. 1992, is still the most useful existing guide to the records that are most likely to help with family history. There are also free leaflets on: *India Office Records. Sources for Family History Research,* IOR Sources for Family History 1, The British Library, [n.d.], and *India Office Records. Ecclesiastical Returns,* The British Library, [n.d.].

25. As most of the Palatines went on to New England or Ireland, the best books available are, not surprisingly, by an American: Hank Z Jones. They are *The Palatine Families of Ireland,* by Henry Z Jones Jr, 2nd ed. Picton Press, Camden, Maine, 1990; *The Palatine Families of New York, 1710* by Henry Z Jones Jr, 2 vols, pub. Henry Z Jones Jr, Universal City, California, 1985; *More Palatine Families,* by Henry Z Jones Jr, pub. Henry Z Jones Jr, Universal City, California, 1991. All these books are effectively biographical dictionaries of the families descended from the original immigrants with details of their origins in Germany.

26. A third edition of the Anglo-German FHS Research Guide Five: *Sugar Bakers,* is in process of publication and gives a detailed description of the process in the mid 19th century, some historical background and descriptions of some of the terrible fires that the business premises were prone to. Some members of the Anglo-German FHS with a particular interest in sugarbakers run a website which contains several thousand entries *(www.mawer.clara.net)* In addition a group of members in Germany is working on an academic work on the patterns of emigration of German sugarbakers which should cast some light on where in Germany they are likely to have come from at different periods. In the period of the Napoleonic Wars, when my own Johan Friedrich Weymann came to London, it appears that sugarbakers are likely to have come from Bremen, Hamburg and northern Hannover.

27. *The German Hospital in London and the Community it served 1845 to 1948,* by Maureen Specht, pub. by the Anglo-German FHS, 1997. While the Hospital's administrative records survive in large quantities and are kept at the Royal Hospitals NHS Trust Archives at St Bartholomews Hospital, West Smithfield, London, EC1, the patients' records do not survive.

28. The Anglo-German FHS is expecting to publish in 2001 a new book on Pork Butchers, giving a detailed historical background to the Germans involvement in this trade. Books are also in preparation on German hairdressers and musicians.

29. Some of the best work on the anti-German hysteria has been written by Panikos Panayi eg. *The Destruction of the German Communities in Britain during the First World War,* by Panikos Panayi, in *Germans in Britain since 1500,* ed. by Panikos Panayi, pub. The Hambledon Press, London, 1996. For the background see also: *German Immigrants in Britain during the Nineteenth Century, 1815-1914,* by Panikos Panayi, pub. Berg, Oxford, 1995.

30. *My German Family in England,* by the founder-president of the Anglo-German FHS, Roy Bernard, pub. Anglo-German FHS, 1991. This describes what happened to one family of German origin which had been settled in London for many years.

31. *Living with the Wire. Civilian internment in the Isle of Man during the two World Wars,* ed. by Yvonne Cresswell, pub. Manx National Heritage, Douglas, 1994. This is a well-illustrated book

accompanying an exhibition put on at the Museum in Douglas in 1994 and is available at the Museum and from the Anglo-German FHS postal bookshop.

32. *Civilian Internment: An insight into Civilian Internment in Britain during WWI,* revised illustrated edition, pub. Anglo-German FHS, 1998. The journal of an internee at Stratford, East London, and Alexandra Palace, by Richard Noschke, and an essay on conditions at Alexandra Palace written by another internee, Rudolf Rocker.

33. *Prisoners of War Information Bureau. List of Places of Internment.* It is available from the Imperial War Museum in London.

34. *Temporary Settlements and Transient Populations. The Legacy of Britain's Prisoner of War Camps: 1940-1948,* by J Anthony Hellen, in Erdkunde, Boss Verlag Kleve, 2000.

35. *Catalogue of Len Metzner Indexes,* compiled by Len Metzner and Pam Freeman, pub. Anglo-German FHS, 2000.

36. *200 Years of the German School in London, 1708-1908,* translated into English by Amanda Price, pub. by the Anglo-German FHS, [n.d.]. A translation of the illustrated booklet published in German in 1908 to commemorate the 200th anniversary of the school. Sadly the school did not survive the First World War.

37. *Etymologisches Worterbuch der Deutschen Familiennamen,* by Prof. J K Brechenmacher, 2 vols, C A Starke-Verlag, Limburg a.d. Lahn, (n.d.), is the best and fullest German surname dictionary available but its coverage of the north of Germany is less complete than of other parts. *Deutsches Namenlexikon,* by Hans Bahlow, Suhrkamp Taschenbuch Verlag, 1985, is less complete but is better for northern German surnames.

38. The *Almanac de Gotha* lists most of the higher nobility but most of the mere von families do not appear. *Genealogisches Handbuch des Adels* covers a larger number of families - see the article: *The Genealogical Handbook of the Nobility: A Guide to German Noble Lineages Past and Present,* by Horst A Reschke in *German Genealogical Digest,* vol 12, no. 4, Winter 1996.

39. See *The German Lineage Book. A Rich Genealogical Source,* by Horst A Reschke in *German Genealogical Digest,* vol 12, no. 2, Summer 1996.

40. See *German Coats of Arms,* by Myron R Falck in *The German Connection,* vol 20, no. 2, Second Quarter 1996.

41. *Armorial Général* by J B Reistap, 2 volumes, 2nd edition, 1885, reprinted by Heraldry Today, 1965; 11 Supplementary volumes also reprinted by Heraldry Today 1965-6; 6 volumes of illustrations reprinted in 3 volumes by Heraldry Today, 1967. A set is in the Society of Genealogists Library and most large reference libraries should have a set.

42. Württemburg emigrants from about 1820 to 1914 are listed in the on-going publication *The Württemburg Emigration Index,* of which seven volumes have been published so far. The Anglo-German FHS has all the volumes and will make a search in them for a small fee. Besides providing the place of origin for the emigrant, they provide the reference necessary to obtain the full application details in the Württemburg Archives at Stuttgart. NB these documents relate to the Kingdom of Württemburg not the Land of Baden-Württemburg. There are several other similar published lists covering eg. the former Duchy of Brunswick and the former Prussian province of Westphalia and the LDS has copies of some of the indexes of the former Grand Duchy of Baden.

43. *Germanic Genealogy: A Guide to World Wide Sources and Migration Patterns,* by Edward R Brandt, Mary Bellingham, Kent Cutkomp, Kermit Frye, & Patricia A Lowe, for the Germanic Genealogy Society, P O Box, 16312, St Paul, MN 55116, USA, 2nd ed. 1997. This volume includes a detailed history of the German-speaking areas of Europe and provides useful historical sketch maps, lists of Societies, archives, etc. As the title implies, however, there is much in this volume on German emigration to other Countries including Australia, New Zealand, and UK. *The German Research Companion,* by Shirley J Riemer, Lorelei Press, P O Box 221356, Sacramento, CA 95822-8356, USA, 2nd revised edition 2000. This volume concentrates more on 1871-1945 Germany and provides even more detail on research resources there. Particularly useful is the full list of addresses of Kreis (ie County) and Town archives. Both volumes, however, have a strong American bias and contain much on research in USA. A slimmer volume that consists principally of addresses is *Useful Addresses for German Research,* Research

Guide Four, Anglo-German FHS, July 2000. It covers Austria and other parts of the former German and Austrian Empires too.

44. *Lands of the German Empire and Before,* by Wendy K Uncapher, pub. Origins, 4327 Milton Avenue, Janesville, WI 53546, USA, January 2000, gives useful histories and "timelines" of the German Empire and of its constituent parts, with outline maps showing the boundaries and the Counties (kreis) or other equivalent divisions. A particularly helpful feature is mapping the various political bodies that covered "Germany" over the last 1,000 years, like the Holy Roman Empire, the Confederation of the Rhine, the North German Confederation, the German Empire and the Weimar Republic. The book is available in UK from the Anglo-German FHS bookshop. There are some useful articles on the geo-political history of particular States in some issues of *German Genealogical Digest:* eg. Baden in *Baden. History and Records,* by Laraine K Ferguson, in vol. 16, no. 4, Winter 2000; Berlin in *Research in Berlin,* by Sonja Hoeke-Nishimoto and Laraine K Ferguson, in vol. 7, no. 4, 4th Quarter 1991; Brandenburg in *A History of Brandenburg* by Larry O Jensen, in vol. 10, no. 3, Fall 1994; Bremen in *Bremen. Emigration, History and Genealogical Records,* by Elizabeth Meiger, in vol. 15, no. 3, Fall 1999; Hesse in *Hessen Areas in Germany* by Larry O Jensen, in vol. 9, no. 3, Autumn 1993; the Palatinate (or Pfalz) in *History of the Palatinate,* by Larry O Jensen, in vol. 6, no. 2, Summer 1990; Prussia in *Prussian Military Records, Part II, Chronology of Brandenburg-Prussia Emphasis on Wars, Leaders and Territorial Changes,* by Laraine K Ferguson, in vol. 15, no. 1, Spring 1999; and Würtemberg in *History of Würtemberg,* by Larry O Jensen in vol. 8, no. 2, 2nd Quarter 1992. Current and back issues of the *German Genealogical Digest* are in the Anglo-German FHS Library in UK but are available by subscription from: German Genealogical Digest, P O Box 112054, Salt Lake City, Utah, 84147, USA.

45. For detailed instructions on how the Catalog is organized for German records see the LDS Research Outline *Germany,* pub. Family History Library, Salt Lake City, Utah, 1994; available in UK from the LDS or from the Anglo-German FHS. This booklet also contains much useful general information on German research. There is another Research

Outline for **Denmark** which is useful if your ancestor came from Schleswig-Holstein or elsewhere in Danish territories.

46. **The German Script,** pub. Verlag Degener & Co, Nurnberger Strasse 27, D91413 Neustadt a.d. Aisch, Germany. **If I Can, You Can Decipher Germanic Records,** by the late Edna M. Bentz, is available in UK from the Anglo-German FHS postal bookshop and the Society of Genealogists' Bookshop.

47. The best gazetteer for the German Empire as it existed 1871-1918 is **Meyers Orts- und Verkehrs-Lexikon des Deutschen Reichs** the 1912 edition of which is now available in a 3 volume set, ed. Raymond S Wright III, from the Genealogical Publishing Co. Inc. Baltimore, Maryland, USA. It contains detailed instructions in English in how to interpret the entries and is well worth the expenditure if you are seriously intending to research in Germany, during the time of the German Empire. The anglo German FHS has a set of Meyers Gazeteer and offers searches to its members. I hope that the GPC will see its way to publishing gazetteers to other parts of Europe like Austria-Hungary.

48. **Letter-Writing Guide: German** pub. Family History Library, Salt Lake City, Utah, USA (also available in UK from the Anglo-German FHS). **Tracing Your German Ancestor** Research Guide Two, Anglo-German FHS, 4th ed. 1998, also contains draft letters that members have used and found helpful in the past.

49. The best guide to the church registers available in English is **German Church Books. Beyond the Basics** by Kenneth L Smith, pub. Picton Press, Camden, Maine, ME 04843-1111, USA. It provides detailed descriptions of the information you can find in the registers with advice on how to solve genealogical problems. Any serious researcher should get a copy.

50. See note 43 above.

51. **Die Ahnenstammkartei des Deutschen volkes: An Introduction and Register,** compiled by Thomas Kent Edlund, pub. LDS Church, 1995. Copy in Anglo-German FHS Library.

52. Immigrant Genealogical Society, P O Box 7369, Burbank, CA 91510-7369, USA. For their website **see feefhs.org/igs.**

53. See **Mecklenburg-Schwerin Census Indexes,** by Peter Towey, in the Anglo-German FHS magazine **Mitteilungsblatt,** No 47, March 1999.

A more detailed article explaining this census is *Mecklenburg Census Records*, by Laraine K Ferguson in *German Genealogical Digest*, vol 8, no. 4, 4th Quarter 1992.

54. See *Census Records in Northern Germany. Part L Schleswig-Holstein*, by Laraine K Ferguson in *German Genealogical Digest*, vol. 6, no. 4, 4th Quarter 1990.

55. A useful booklet, in English, is *German Military Records as Genealogical Sources* by Horst A Reschke, and available from him at P O Box 27161, Salt Lake City, UT 84127-0161, USA. This is very short, 12 pages, but lists the armies of the different States and the archives where they are kept, explains the background and gives a bibliography. *Useful Addresses for German Research,* also contains details of army records held at the various German State Archives. A number of articles on military research at different periods appears in *The German Connection,* vol 20, no. 3, Third Quarter 1996. Also of interest are the articles: *Beginning your Military Research,* by Mr Reschke and: *German Military Records. History and Genealogical Records. Part I: The Wars of Unification,* by Laraine K Ferguson in *German Genealogical Digest,* vol 11, no. 2, Summer 1995.

56. The main listing of Military Church Books is *Verzeichnis der Militarkirchenbucher in der Bundesrepublick Deutschland (nach dem Stand vom 30 September 1990) [List of the Military Church Books in the Federal Republic of Germany (as of 30 September 1990)],* by Wolfgang Eger, pub. Verlag Degener & Co, Neustadt a.d. Aisch, Germany, 1993. This volume only covers those books held in the former West Germany and about 650 volumes stored in Leipzig. The Church Books held in the rest of the former East Germany and elsewhere in the former German territories in Eastern Europe have not yet been listed A useful article, in *The German Connection,* vol 20, no. 3, Third Quarter 1996, is *A Guide to Military Churchbooks* by Merriam M Moore which explains in English how to use the above *Verzeichnis* ... and the history of what has happened to the churchbooks since 1945. As an example of successful research using the Prussian churchbooks, together with a detailed history and explanation of the Prussian "cantonal" recruiting system, see *Prussia's Military Records. The Officers and Soldiers of Berlin,*

by Laraine Kowallis Ferguson, in *German Genealogical Digest,* vol. 14, no. 4, Winter 1998.

57. The Anglo-German FHS has copies of two German Army Ranglisten, for 1906 and 1918, which includes the Württemburg Army, and the Bavarian Army Ranglist for 1918 and will make searches in them for a small fee. They can still be bought in second-hand bookshops in Germany.

58. For details of the Leipzig police records see *Leipzig, Saxony. Genealogical Collections & Historical and Cultural Insights,* by Laraine K Ferguson in *German Genealogical Digest,* vol 12, no. 2, Summer 1996.

59. For details of the Hamburg police records see the two articles both entitled *Hamburg Police Records* by Sonja Hoeke-Nashimoto in *German Genealogical Digest,* vol 6, nos. 1 & 2. 1st & 2nd Quarters, 1990. The first article provides an index to the LDS microfilms of male and female non-citizen (ie not full Citizens of Hamburg) residents of Hamburg 1868-1889. The second article gives indexes to the microfilms of the passport records 1851-1929.

60. See *Dorfsippenbuccher and Ortssippenbuccher,* by Larry O Jensen, in *German Genealogical Digest,* vol VII, no. 2, 2nd Quarter 1991 for an outline. A full list of the Salt Lake City holdings can be found in their Catalog CD-ROM but, in the case of microfilmed books, they are not usually willing to send a copy to Europe for copyright reasons. A complete listing of the extensive holdings of the Deutsche Zentralstelle fur Genealogie, Leipzig, is published as *Ortsfamilienbucher mit Standort Leipcig,* by the Zentralstelle. The most recent edition pub. in 2000 lists their holdings of these books as at Autumn 1998. A further listing of the books and articles received from then to Spring 2000 was published in the bimonthly magazine *Genealogie. Deutsche Zeitschrift fur Familienkunde,* Heft 11/12, Band XXV, Nov-Dez 2000, pp 387-406.

61. See *Citizenship Records,* by Gerhard Jeske, in *German Genealogical Digest,* vol. 16, no. 3, Fall 2000.

62. See *Useful Addresses for German Research* . A more detailed book is *A Genealogical Guide to research ancestors from East German and Sudeten German areas, from German resettlement regions in Central, Eastern and South-eastern Europe.* This is published

for a German family history society, AGoFF - Arbeitgemeinschaft Ostdeutscher Familienforscher e. V., as an English translation of their main handbook *Wegweiser.* The most recent edition of the English translation is 1998 but the German language version on which it was based, and thus the information in it, was dated 1995. A new German language version is expected in early 2001 and, if you can get by with that, it would be more useful than the 1998 English version. The publisher is Verlag Degener & Co, D-91403 Neustadt a.d. Aisch, Germany. The book contains detailed lists of archives, homeland collections, etc. for every kreis or county in the former German Empire east of the Oder-Neisse line, and other areas of German settlement in Europe, with useful maps, potted histories and addresses.

63. See *Useful Addresses for German Research.* There is a useful article on these records, and the microfilm of them held by the LDS Library, in *Immigration Records of the EWZ* in *FEEFHS Quarterly,* vol VI, nos. 1-4, 1998, which also includes an alphabetical listing of the LDS microfilm numbers for the card index and the subsequent case files.

64. See note 62 above. There is also a useful book: *Polish Roots,* by Rosemary A Chorzempa, the Genealogical Publishing Co. Inc. 1001 N. Calvert St, Baltimore, Maryland, 21202, USA, 1993. She covers the Ukraine as well, gives draft phrases in Polish and advice on writing to Poland. See also note 43 above.

65. See note 62 above.

66. See *Vienna City Records,* by Steven W Blodgett, in *FEEFHS Journal,* vol. VIII, 2000.

67. See note 43 above.

68. For addresses see note 43 above.

69. See the LDS Research Outline: *Denmark* available from LDS libraries, and *Genealogical Guidebook & Atlas of Denmark,* by Frank Smith & Finn A Thomsen, Thomsen's Genealogical Centre, P O Box 588, Bountiful, Utah 84010, USA, 4th edition, 1998. The latter contains useful maps of the administrative areas of Denmark at different times and a gazetteer of parishes and other places.

70. *Colony of Heligoland (Helgoland). Census 5 April 1881 (C0122/3 7),* Record Series Four, Anglo-German FHS, pub. 1999 [on 2 fiches with an index].

71. See *Useful Addresses for German Research,* which lists all the German, and some other European and American, family history societies, and note 43 above.